The cherished Book of Psalms is part of the Old Testament but many of the songs and prayers are quoted in the New Testament.

These deeply moving religious poems have been used as a book of worship by the Christian church from its earliest beginnings.

THE PSALMS FOR MODERN MAN
IN TODAY'S ENGLISH VERSION
was originally published by the
American Bible Society.

THE
PSALMS

for Modern Man

Today's English Version

PUBLISHED BY POCKET BOOKS NEW YORK

THE PSALMS FOR MODERN MAN in Today's English Version
American Bible Society edition published December, 1970
POCKET BOOK edition published May, 1972

This portion of Holy Scripture in Today's English Version is a part of the Old Testament of the Bible. We urge you next to read the entire New Testament, which may be secured from your church, religious bookstore or the American Bible Society.

This POCKET BOOK edition includes every word contained in the original edition. POCKET BOOK editions are published by POCKET BOOKS, a division of Simon & Schuster, Inc., 630 Fifth Avenue, New York, N.Y. 10020. Trademarks registered in the United States and other countries.

L

PREFACE

The book of Psalms is the hymnbook and prayer book of the Bible. Composed by different authors over a long period of time, these hymns and prayers were collected and used by the people of Israel in their worship, and eventually this collection was included in their Holy Scriptures.

These religious poems are of many kinds: there are hymns of praise and worship of God; prayers for help, protection, and salvation; pleas for forgiveness; songs of thanksgiving for God's blessings; and petitions for the punishment of enemies. These prayers are personal and national; some portray the most intimate feelings of one person, while others represent the needs and feelings of all the people of God.

Many of the Psalms are quoted in the New Testament, and such passages as Mary's song of praise (Luke 1.46-55), Zechariah's prophecy (Luke 1.68-79), and Simeon's prayer of thanksgiving (Luke 2.29-32) reflect the language and style of the psalms. They were used by Jesus, quoted by the writers of the New Testament, and became the treasured book of worship of the Christian Church from its very beginning.

This translation of the Psalms attempts to represent the meaning of the Hebrew text as faithfully as possible, and at the same time convey something of the grace and beauty of the original poetry. The basic poetic structure of the Psalms consists of a statement which is repeated, in a modified fashion, in the next line. Sometimes this parallelism is continued over several lines. The possible variations are almost unlimited, and the reader who is aware of them will discover new beauty in the Psalms. In addition, unusual words and figurative expressions help create and sustain a poetic atmosphere.

Ancient Hebrew poetry did not have rhyme, and the meter was quite different from what is commonly used in English. This translation has been made in free verse, and the translators have tried to put the Psalms in easy-flowing, rhythmical lines that can be effective in public worship as well as in private devotion.

Like the New Testament in Today's English Version, this is a distinctly new translation that does not conform to traditional vocabulary or style, but seeks to express the meaning of the Hebrew text in words and forms accepted as standard by people everywhere who employ English as a means of communication. Where there is general agreement that the Hebrew text presents unresolved difficulties in interpretation, this translation employs the evidence of other ancient texts or follows present-day scholarly consensus. All such modifications are identified in footnotes.

This text was prepared by a committee working on a translation of the entire Old Testament. It was submitted to Bible scholars and stylists for study and comment, and was finally reviewed and approved by the Translations Committee of the American Bible Society. The line drawings were especially prepared to accompany the text.

THE PSALMS

BOOK ONE
(Psalms 1—41)

True Happiness

1 Happy is the man
　who refuses the advice of evil men,
who does not follow the example of
　sinners,
or join those who make fun of
　God.
2 Instead, he enjoys reading the law of the
　Lord,
　and studying it day and night.
3 He is like a tree that grows beside a
　stream;
　it gives fruit at the right time,
　and its leaves do not dry up.
He succeeds in everything he does.

4 But evil men are not like this at all;
　they are like straw that the wind blows
　　away.
5 Evil men will be condemned by God;
　sinners will be kept apart from the right-
　　eous.
6 The Lord cares for the righteous man,
　but the evil man will be lost forever.

God's Chosen King

2 Why do the nations plan rebellion?
　Why do these people make useless
　　plots?
2 Their kings revolt,
　their rulers plot together
　against the Lord and his chosen king.

³ "Let us free ourselves from their rule,"
    they say;
    "let us throw off their control."

⁴ From his throne in heaven the Lord
    laughs
    and makes fun of them.
⁵ He speaks to them in anger,
    and terrifies them with his fury.
⁶ "On Zion, my sacred hill," he says,
    "I have installed my king."

⁷ "I will announce what the Lord declared,"
    says the king.
    "The Lord said to me: 'You are my son;
    today I have become your father.
⁸ Ask, and I will give you all the nations;
    the whole earth will be yours.
⁹ You will rule over them with an iron hand;
    you will break them in pieces like a clay
        pot.' "

¹⁰ Now listen to me, you kings;
    pay attention, you rulers!
¹¹ Serve the Lord with fear;
    tremble ¹² and bow down to him;ᵃ
or else he will be angry, and you will die,
    for his anger is quickly aroused.
Happy are all who go to him for protec-
    tion!

Morning Prayer for Helpᵇ

3 I have so many enemies, Lord,
        so many who turn against me!
² They talk about me and say,
    "God will not help him!"

³ But you, Lord, always shield me from
    danger;

ᵃ*Hebrew unclear.* ᵇ*Hebrew title:* David wrote this psalm after he ran
away from his son Absalom.

you give me victory
and restore my courage.
⁴ I call to the Lord for help,
and from his sacred hill he answers me.

Always shield me from danger

⁵ I lie down and sleep,
and I wake up safe, because the Lord
protects me.
⁶ I am not afraid of the thousands of
enemies
who surround me on every side.

⁷ Come, Lord! Save me, my God!
You defeat all my enemies,
you destroy all the wicked.
⁸ Salvation comes from the Lord—
may he bless his people!

Evening Prayer for Help

4 Answer me when I call,
God, my defender!
When I was in trouble, you came to my
help.
Be kind to me now and hear my prayer!

² How long will you men insult me?
    How long will you love what is worth-
       less,
    and go after what is false?

³ Remember that the Lord has chosen me
     to be his own,
    and hears me when I call to him.

⁴ Be afraid and stop your sinning;
    think deeply about this,
    alone and silent in your rooms.
⁵ Offer the right sacrifices to the Lord,
    and put your trust in him.

⁶ There are many who say,
    "How we wish to receive a blessing!"
Look on us with kindness, Lord!
⁷ The joy that you give me is much greater
    than the joy of those who have plenty of
     grain and wine.

⁸ As soon as I lie down, I go quietly to sleep;
    you alone, Lord, keep me perfectly safe.

A Prayer for Protection

5   Listen to my words, Lord,
     and hear my sighs.
² My king and my God,
    listen to my cry for help.

  I will pray to you, Lord;
³   in the morning you hear my voice;
    at sunrise I offer up my prayer,
    and wait for your answer.

⁴ You are not a God who is pleased with
     wrongdoing;
    you allow no evil in your presence.

5 You cannot stand the sight of proud men;
    you hate all wicked men.
6 You destroy all liars,
    and despise violent and deceitful men.

7 As for me, I can come into your house,
    because of your great love;
  I can worship in your holy temple,
    and bow down to you in reverence.
8 Lord, I have many enemies;
    lead me to do your will,
      and make your way plain for me to
        follow!

9 What my enemies say can never be
      trusted;
    they only want to destroy;
  their mouth is like an open grave,
    and their words are smooth and decep-
      tive.
10 Condemn and punish them, God;
    cause their evil plans to fail.
  Throw them out of your presence
    because of their many sins
    and their rebellion against you.

11 All who find safety in you will rejoice;
    they will always sing for joy.
  You protect those who love you;
    because of you they are truly happy.
12 You bless those who obey you, Lord;
    your kindness protects them like a
      shield.

A Prayer for Help in Time of Trouble

6 Lord, don't be angry and rebuke me!
    Don't punish me in your anger!
2 Have pity on me, because I am worn out;
    restore me, because I am completely
      exhausted;

³ my whole being is deeply troubled.
How long, Lord, will this last?

⁴ Come and save me, Lord;
    because you love me, rescue me from
        death.
⁵ In the world of the dead you are not
        remembered;
    no one can praise you there!

⁶ I am worn out with grief;
    every night my bed is damp from my
        crying,
    my pillow is soaked with tears.
⁷ My eyes are swollen from so much weep-
        ing,
    and I can hardly see—
    all because of my enemies!

⁸ Go away, you evildoers!
The Lord hears my weeping;
⁹   he listens to my cries for help,
    and answers my prayers.
¹⁰ My enemies will all know the bitter shame
        of defeat;
    in utter confusion they will suddenly be
        driven away.

A Prayer for Justice*c*

7 Lord, my God, I have found safety with
        you;
    save me, and rescue me from all who
        pursue me,
² or else like a lion they will carry me off
    where no one can save me;
    and there they will tear me to pieces.

³ Lord, my God, if I have done any of these:

cHebrew title: A song which David sang to the Lord because of Cush
the Benjaminite.

if I have wronged someone,
4 if I have betrayed my friend,
　or without cause done violence to my
　　enemy,
5 then may my enemies pursue me and
　catch me,
　may they cut me down and kill me,
　and leave me lifeless on the ground!

6 Rise in your anger, Lord,
　and stand up against the fury of my
　　enemies!
Wake up and help me,
　because justice is what you demand.
7 Bring together all the peoples around you,
　and rule over them from above.*d*
8 You, Lord, are the judge of all men.
　Judge in my favor,
　because I am innocent and good.

9 Stop the wickedness of evil men,
　and reward, I pray, the good men.
You are a righteous God,
　and judge men's thoughts and desires.
10 God is my protector;
　he saves those who obey him.
11 God is a righteous judge
　and always condemns the wicked.

12 If men do not repent,
　God will sharpen his sword.
He bends his bow and makes it ready;
13 　he takes up his deadly weapons
　and aims his burning arrows.

14 See how the wicked man thinks up evil;
　he plans trouble and practices decep-
　　tion.
15 He digs a deep hole in the ground,
　then falls into his own pit!

---

*d*rule over them from above; *Hebrew* return above over them.

¹⁶ So he is punished by his own evil;
      he is hurt by his own violence.

¹⁷ I will thank the Lord for his justice,
      I will sing praises to the Lord, the Most
         High.

God's Glory and Man's Dignity

8   Lord, our Lord,
         your greatness is seen in all the
            world!
   Your praise reaches up to the heavens;
²   it is sung by children and babies.
   You have built a fortress against your foes
      to stop your enemies and adversaries.

³ When I look at the sky, which you have
      made,
      at the moon and the stars, which you set
         in their places—
⁴ what is man, that you think of him;
      mere man, that you care for him?

⁵ Yet you made him inferior only to your-
      self;
      you crowned him with glory and honor.
⁶ You made him ruler over all you have
      made;
      you placed him over all things:
⁷ sheep and cattle, and wild animals too;
⁸   the birds and the fish,
      and all the creatures in the seas.

⁹ Lord, our Lord,
      your greatness is seen in all the world!

Thanksgiving to God for His Justice

9   I will praise you, Lord, with all my
            heart,
      I will tell all the wonderful things you
         have done.

Your greatness is seen in all the world!

² I will sing with joy because of you.
   I will sing praise to you, Most High!

³ My enemies turn back when you appear;
   they fall down and die.
⁴ As a righteous judge you sit on your
      throne,
   and you have judged in my favor.

⁵ You have condemned the heathen and
      destroyed the wicked,
   and they will be remembered no more.
⁶ Our enemies are finished forever;
   you have destroyed their cities,
   and they are completely forgotten.

⁷ But the Lord is king forever;
   he has set up his throne for judgment.
⁸ He rules the world with righteousness;
   he judges the people with justice.

⁹ The Lord is a refuge for the oppressed,
   a place of safety in times of trouble.
¹⁰ Those who know you, Lord, will trust you;

you do not abandon anyone who comes
to you.

11 Sing praise to the Lord, who rules in Zion!
Tell every nation what he has done!
12 God remembers those who suffer;
he does not forget their cry,
and he punishes those who wrong them.

13 Be merciful to me, Lord!
See how mistreated I am by those who
hate me!
Rescue me from death, Lord,
14 that I may stand before the people of
Jerusalem
and tell them all the things for which I
praise you.
I will rejoice because you saved me.

15 The heathen have dug a pit and fallen in;
they have set a trap and been caught in
it.
16 The Lord has revealed himself by his righteous judgments,
and the wicked are trapped by their
own deeds.

17 Death is the destiny of all the wicked,
of all those who reject God.
18 The needy will not always be neglected;
the hope of the oppressed will not be
crushed forever.

19 Come, Lord! Don't let men defy you!
Bring the heathen before you and judge
them.
20 Make them afraid, Lord;
make them know that they are only
men.

A Prayer for Help

10   Why are you so far away, Lord?
        Why do you hide yourself in times
           of trouble?
2 The wicked are proud and persecute the
        poor;
     may they be caught in the traps they
        have made.

3 The wicked man brags about his evil
        desires;
     the greedy man curses and rejects the
        Lord.
4 In his pride the wicked man says,
     "God will not punish me! He doesn't
        care!"
   This is what the wicked man thinks.

5 He succeeds in all he does.
     He cannot understand God's judg-
        ments;
     he sneers at his enemies.
6 He says to himself, "I will never fail;
     I will never be in trouble."
7 His speech is filled with curses, lies, and
        threats;
     he is quick to speak hateful and evil
        words.

8 He hides himself in the villages;
     he waits there and murders innocent
        people.
   He spies on his helpless victim;
9   he waits in his hiding place like a lion.
   He lies in wait for his victim;
     he catches him in his trap and drags him
        away.

10 The helpless victim lies crushed;
     brute strength has defeated him.
11 The wicked man says to himself, "God
        doesn't care!

He has closed his eyes, and will never
see me!"

¹² Come, Lord, and save me!
Don't forget the oppressed, God!
¹³ How can the wicked man despise God,
and say to himself, "He will not punish
me"?

¹⁴ But you do see; you take notice of suffering and grief
and are always ready to help.
The helpless man commits himself to you,
because you have always helped the
needy.

¹⁵ Break the power of wicked and evil men;
punish them for their wickedness,
until their punishment is complete.

¹⁶ The Lord is king forever and ever,
and the heathen will disappear from his
land.

¹⁷ You will listen, Lord, to the prayers of the
lowly;
you will give them courage.
¹⁸ You will hear the cries of the oppressed
and the orphans
and judge in their favor,
so that mortal men may cause terror no
more.

Confidence in the Lord

11   I trust in the Lord for safety.
How foolish of you to say to me,
"Fly away like a bird to the mountains,
²   because the wicked draw their bows
and aim their arrows
to shoot at good men in the darkness.

³ There is nothing a good man can do
  when things fall apart."

⁴ The Lord is in his holy temple;
  he has his throne in heaven.
He watches all men
  and knows what they do.
⁵ He examines both the good and the
    wicked;
  he hates the lawless with all his heart.

⁶ He sends down flaming coalsᵉ and burning
    sulphur on the wicked;
  he punishes them with a scorching
    flame.
⁷ The Lord is righteous and loves good
    deeds;
  those who obey him will live in his
    presence.

A Prayer for Help

12   Save me, Lord!
        There are no good men left,
    and honest men can no longer be found.
² All men lie to one another,
    and deceive each other with flattery.

³ Silence those flattering tongues, Lord,
    and close those boastful mouths!
⁴ They say, "We will speak as we wish,
    and no one will stop us.
    Who can tell us what to say?"

⁵ "But now I will come," says the Lord,
    "because the needy are oppressed,
    and the persecuted groan in pain.
  I will give them the security they long
    for!"

ᵉOne ancient translation coals; Hebrew traps.

⁶ The Lord's promises can be trusted;
    they are as genuine as silver,
    refined seven times in the furnace.

⁷ Keep us always safe, Lord,
    and preserve us from such people.
⁸ Wicked men are everywhere,
    and everyone praises what is evil.

A Prayer for Help

13 How long will you forget me, Lord?
        Forever?
    How much longer will you hide your-
        self from me?
² How long must I endure pain?ᶠ
    How long will sorrow fill my heart day
        and night?
    How long will my enemies triumph
        over me?

³ Look at me, Lord my God, and answer
        me.
    Restore my strength, so that I will not
        die.
⁴ Then my enemies cannot say, "We have
        defeated him!"
    They cannot be glad over my downfall.

⁵ But I rely on your constant love;
    I will be glad, because you will save me.
⁶ I will sing to the Lord,
    because he has been good to me.

The Wickedness of Men

(Psalm 53)

14 Fools say to themselves,
        "God doesn't matter!"
    They are all corrupt,

___

ᶠOne ancient translation endure pain; Hebrew make plans.

they have done terrible things;
    there is no one who does what is right.

2 The Lord looks down at men from heaven
    to see if there are any who are wise,
    any who worship him.
3 But they have all gone wrong,
    they are all equally bad;
 not one of them does what is right,
    not a single one.

4 "Don't they know?" asks the Lord.
    "Are all these evildoers ignorant?
They live by robbing my people
    and do not pray to me."

5 But they will become terrified,
    because God is with those who obey
    him.
6 They make fun of the plans of the helpless
    man,
    because he trusts in the Lord.

7 How I pray that salvation
    will come to Israel from Zion!
When the Lord makes his people prosper-
    ous again,
    Jacob's descendants will be happy;
    the people of Israel will be glad.

What God Requires

15 Lord, who may live in your temple?
    Who may stay on Zion, your sa-
    cred hill?

2 The man who obeys God in everything,
    and always does what is right;
whose words are true and sincere,
3   and who does not slander others.
He does no wrong to his friends
    and does not spread rumors about his
    neighbors.

⁴ He despises those whom God rejects,
    but honors those who obey the Lord.
He always does what he promises,
    no matter how much it may cost him.
⁵ He makes loans without charging interest
    and cannot be bribed to testify against
    the innocent.

He who does these things will never fail.

A Prayer of Confidence

16   Protect me, God, because I come to
    you for safety.
² I say to the Lord, "You are my Lord;
    all the good things I have come from
    you."

³ How excellent are the Lord's faithful peo-
    ple!*g*
    My greatest pleasure is to be with them.

⁴ Those who rush to other gods
    bring many troubles on themselves.*g*
I will not take part in their sacrifices;
    I will not worship their gods.

⁵ You, Lord, are all I have,
    and you give me all I need;
    my life is in your hands.
⁶ How wonderful are your gifts to me;
    how good they are!

⁷ I praise the Lord, because he guides me,
    and in the night my conscience warns
    me.
⁸ I am always aware of the Lord's presence;
    he is near, and nothing can shake me.

⁹ And so I am full of happiness and joy,
    and I always feel secure;

g Hebrew unclear.

10 because you will not allow me to go to the
    world of the dead,
  you will not abandon to the depths be-
    low the one you love.

11 You will show me the path that leads to
    life;
  your presence fills me with joy,
  and your help brings pleasure forever.

The Prayer of an Innocent Man

17   Listen, Lord, to my righteous plea;
       pay attention to my cry for help!
  Listen to my prayer,
    because there is no deceit in me.
2 You will judge in my favor,
    because you know what is right.

3 You know my heart;
    you come to me at night.
  You have examined me completely
    and found no evil desire in me;
    I speak no evil, 4as others do;
  I have obeyed your command
    and have not followed*h* the path of vio-
    lence.
5 I have always walked in your way
    and have not strayed from it.

6 I pray to you, God, because you answer
    me;
    so turn to me and listen to my words.
7 Reveal your wonderful love, Savior;
    at your side we are safe from our ene-
    mies.

8 Protect me, as you would your very eyes;
    hide me in the shadow of your wings
9   from the attacks of the wicked.

h One ancient translation have not followed; *Hebrew* have followed.

My enemies, full of hate, surround me;
10   they have no pity and speak proudly.
11 Now they are around me wherever I turn,
     watching for a chance to pull me down.
12 They are like lions, wanting to tear me to
       pieces,
     like young lions, waiting for me in their
       hiding places.

13 Come, Lord, oppose my enemies and de-
     feat them!
Save me from the wicked by your sword;
14 save me from them by your power,
     from those who in this life have all they
       want.
Punish them with the sufferings you have
     stored up for them;
     may there be enough for their children,
     and some left over for their children's
       children!

15 Because I am righteous, I will see you,
     and when I awake, your presence will
       fill me with joy.

David's Song of Victory[i]
(2 Samuel 22.1–51)

18   How I love you, Lord!
       You are my defender.
2 The Lord is my Savior;
     he is my strong fortress.
My God is my protection,
     and I am safe with him.
He protects me like a shield;
     he defends me and keeps me safe.
3 I call to the Lord,
     and he saves me from my enemies.
Praise the Lord!

[i]*Hebrew title:* These are the words that David, the Lord's servant,
sang to the Lord on the day the Lord saved him from Saul and all
his other enemies.

⁴Death pulled its ropes tight around me;
  the waves of destruction rolled over me.
⁵Death pulled its ropes tight around me,
  and the grave set its trap for me.

⁶In my trouble I called to the Lord;
  I called to my God for help.
In his temple he heard my voice;
  my cry for help reached his ears.

⁷Then the earth trembled and shook;
    the foundations of the mountains
    rocked and quivered,
    because God was angry!
⁸Smoke poured out of his nostrils,
    a consuming flame and burning coals
    from his mouth.
⁹He pulled back the sky and came down,
    with a dark cloud under his feet.
¹⁰He flew down on the backs of the cheru-
    bim;
    he traveled swiftly on the wings of the
    wind.
¹¹He covered himself with darkness;
    thick clouds, full of water, were around
    him.
¹²Hailstones and flaming coals
    came from the lightning before him
    and broke through the dark clouds.

¹³Then the Lord thundered from the sky;
    and the voice of the Most High was
    heard.ʲ
¹⁴He shot his arrows, and scattered his ene-
    mies;
    with flashes of lightning he sent them
    running.
¹⁵The bottom of the ocean was revealed,

ʲOne ancient translation (and see 2 Sam. 22.14) was heard; *Hebrew*
adds hailstones and flaming coals.

and the foundations of the earth were
    uncovered,
when you rebuked your enemies, Lord,
    and roared at them in anger.

16 The Lord reached down from heaven and
        took hold of me;
    he pulled me out of the deep waters.
17 He rescued me from my powerful ene-
        mies,
    and from all those who hate me—
    they were too strong for me!
18 When I was in trouble they attacked me,
    but the Lord protected me.
19 He helped me out of danger;
    he saved me because he was pleased
        with me.

20 The Lord rewards me because I am right-
        eous;
    he blesses me because I am innocent.
21 I have obeyed the law of the Lord;
    I have not rebelled against my God.
22 I have observed all his laws;
    I have not disobeyed his commands.
23 He knows that I am faultless,
    that I have kept myself from evil.
24 And so he rewards me because I am right-
        eous,
    because he knows that I am innocent.

25 You, Lord, are faithful to those who are
        faithful,
    and completely good to those who are
        perfect.
26 You are pure to those who are pure,
    but hostile to those who are wicked.
27 You save those who are humble,
    but you humble those who are proud.

28 The Lord gives me light;
    my God dispels my darkness.

²⁹ He gives me strength to attack my enemies,
    the power to overcome their defenses.

³⁰ This God—how perfect are his deeds,
    how dependable are his words!
He is like a shield
    for all who seek his protection.

³¹ The Lord alone is God;
    God alone is our defense.
³² He is the God who makes me strong,
    who makes my pathway safe.
³³ He makes me surefooted as a deer;
    he keeps me safe on the mountains.
³⁴ He trains me for battle,
    so that I can use the strongest bow.

³⁵ You, Lord, protect me and save me;
    your care has made me great,
    and your power has kept me safe.
³⁶ You have kept me from being captured,
    and I have never fallen.
³⁷ I chase my enemies and catch them;
    I do not stop until I defeat them.
³⁸ I strike them down, and they cannot rise;
    they lie defeated at my feet.
³⁹ You give me strength for the battle
    and victory over my enemies.
⁴⁰ You make my enemies run from me;
    I destroy those who hate me.
⁴¹ They cry for help, but no one can save
them;
    they call to the Lord, but he does not
    answer.
⁴² I crush them, so that they become like
dust,
    which the wind blows away.
I trample on them, like mud in the streets.

⁴³ You save me from a rebellious people,
    and make me ruler over the nations;

people I did not know are now my sub-
    jects.
⁴⁴ When they hear me they obey;
    foreigners bow before me.
⁴⁵ They lose their courage
    and come trembling from their for-
    tresses.

⁴⁶ The Lord lives! Praise my defender!
    God is my Savior! Proclaim his great-
    ness!
⁴⁷ He gives me victory over my enemies;
    he subdues the peoples under me
⁴⁸   and saves me from my foes.

You, Lord, give me victory over my ene-
    mies
    and protect me from violent men.
⁴⁹ And so I will praise you among the na-
    tions;
    I will sing praise to you.

⁵⁰ God gives great victories to his king;
    he shows constant love to the one he
    has chosen,
    to David and his descendants forever.

God's Glory in Creation

19 How clearly the sky reveals God's
        glory!
    How plainly it shows what he has done!
² Each day announces it to the following
    day;
    each night repeats it to the next.
³ No speech or words are used,
    no sound is heard;
⁴ yet their voiceᵏ goes out to all the world,
    their message reaches the ends of the
    earth.

ᵏ*Some ancient translations* voice; *Hebrew* line.

God set up a tent in the sky for the sun;
5   it comes out like a bridegroom striding
      from his house,
    like an athlete, eager to run a race.
6 It starts at one end of the sky
    and goes around to the other.
    Nothing can hide from its heat.

The Law of the Lord

7 The law of the Lord is perfect;
    it gives new life.
The commands of the Lord are trust-
    worthy,
    giving wisdom to those who lack it.
8 The rules of the Lord are right,
    and those who obey them are happy.
His commandments are completely just
    and give understanding to the mind.
9 The worship of the Lord is good;
    it will continue forever.
The judgments of the Lord are just,
    they are always fair.
10 They are more desirable than gold,
    even the finest gold.
They are sweeter than honey,
    even the purest honey.
11 They give knowledge to me, your servant;
    I am rewarded for obeying them.

12 No one can see his own errors;
    deliver me from hidden faults!
13 Keep me safe, also, from open sins;
    don't let them rule over me.
Then I shall be perfect
    and free from terrible sin.

14 May my words and my thoughts be ac-
    ceptable to you,
    O Lord, my refuge and my redeemer!

A Prayer for Victory

20 May the Lord answer you in the day
of trouble!
May the God of Jacob protect you!
2 May he send you help from his temple
and give you aid from Mount Zion!
3 May he accept all your offerings
and be pleased with all your sacrifices.
4 May he give you what you desire
and make all your plans succeed.
5 Then we will shout for joy over your victory
and celebrate your triumph by praising
our God.
May the Lord answer all your requests!

6 Now I know that the Lord gives victory to
his chosen king;
he answers him from his holy heaven,
and by his great power makes him victorious.
7 Some trust in their war chariots,
and others in their horses,
but we trust in the power of the Lord
our God!
8 They will stumble and fall,
but we will rise and stand firm!

9 Give victory to the king, Lord;
the Lord will answer us when we call.

Praise for Victory

21 The king is glad, Lord, because you
gave him strength;
he is full of joy, because you made him
victorious.
2 You have given him what he wanted;
you have answered his request.

3 You came to him with great blessings
and set a gold crown on his head.

⁴ He asked for life, and you gave it;
  a long and lasting life.

⁵ His glory is great because of your help;
  you have given him fame and majesty.
⁶ Your blessings are upon him forever,
  and your presence fills him with gladness.

⁷ The king trusts in the Most High;
  and because of the Lord's constant love
  he will be king forever.
⁸ The king will catch all his enemies;
  he will capture all those who hate him.
⁹ He will destroy them like a blazing fire,
  when he appears.

  The Lord will devour them in his anger,
  and fire will consume them.
¹⁰ The king will kill all their children;
  he will slaughter all their descendants.

¹¹ They make evil plans and plot against
   him,
   but they will not succeed.
¹² He will shoot his arrows at them,
   and make them turn and run.

¹³ Come, Lord, with your strength!
   We will sing and praise your power.

A Cry of Anguish and a Song of Praise

22   My God, my God, why have you
        abandoned me?
   I have cried desperately for help,
     but it still does not come!
² During the day I call to you, my God,
   but you do not answer;
   I call at night,
   but get no rest.
³ But you are enthroned as the Holy One,
   the one whom Israel praises.

⁴ Our ancestors put their trust in you;
  they trusted you, and you saved them.
⁵ They called to you and escaped from dan-
    ger;
  they trusted in you and were not disap-
    pointed.

⁶ But I am no longer a man; I am a worm,
  despised and scorned by all!
⁷ All who see me make fun of me;
  they stick out their tongues and shake
    their heads.
⁸ "You relied on the Lord," they say. "Why
    doesn't he save you?
  If the Lord likes you, why doesn't he
    help you?"

⁹ It was you who brought me safely through
    birth,
  and when I was a baby you kept me
    safe.
¹⁰ I have relied on you ever since I was born;
  since my birth you have been my God.
¹¹ Do not stay away from me!
  Trouble is near,
  and there is no one to help.

¹² Many enemies surround me like bulls;
  they are all around me,
  like fierce bulls from the land of Bashan.
¹³ They open their mouths like lions,
  roaring and tearing at me.

¹⁴ My strength is gone,
  gone like water spilled on the ground.
  All my bones are out of joint;
  my heart feels like melted wax inside
    me.
¹⁵ My throat[l] is as dry as dust,
  and my tongue sticks to the roof of my
    mouth.
  You have left me for dead in the dust.

---

[l]My throat: *Hebrew* My strength.

¹⁶ A gang of evil men is around me;
   like a pack of dogs, they close in on me;
   they tear^m my hands and feet.
¹⁷ All my bones can be seen.
  My enemies look at me and stare;
¹⁸   they divide my clothes among them-
     selves
   and gamble for my robe.

Hurry and help me, my Savior!

¹⁹ Don't stay away from me, Lord!
   Hurry and help me, my Savior!
²⁰ Save me from the sword;
   save my life from those dogs.
²¹ Rescue me from those lions;
   I am helplessⁿ before those wild bulls.

²² I will tell my people what you have done;
   I will praise you in their meeting:
²³ "Praise him, you servants of the Lord!
   Honor him, you descendants of Jacob;
   worship him, you people of Israel!
²⁴ He does not neglect the poor or ignore
   their suffering;

---

^m*Some ancient translations* they tear; *others* they tie; *Hebrew* like a
lion.   ⁿ*Some ancient translations* I am helpless; *Hebrew* you answered me.

he does not keep away from them,
but answers when they call for help."

25 In the full assembly I will praise you for
what you have done;
in the presence of all who obey you
I will offer the sacrifices I promised.
26 The poor will eat as much as they want;
those who come to the Lord will praise
him.
May they prosper forever!

27 All nations will remember the Lord;
from every part of the world they will
turn to him;
all races will worship him.
28 The Lord is king,
and he rules over the nations.

29 All proud men will bow down to him;*o*
all mortal men will bow down before
him,
all those who are bound to die.
30 Future generations will serve him;
men will speak of the Lord to the coming generation.*p*

31 People not yet born will be told:
"The Lord saved his people!"

The Lord Our Shepherd

23   The Lord is my shepherd;
I have everything I need.
2 He lets me rest in fields of green grass
and leads me to quiet pools of fresh
water.
3 He gives me new strength.

---

*o*will bow down to him: *Hebrew* will eat and bow down.   *pOne
ancient translation* to the coming generation; *Hebrew* to the generation. They will come.

He guides me in the right way,
   as he has promised.
4 Even if that way goes through deepest
   darkness,
   I will not be afraid, Lord,
   because you are with me!
Your shepherd's rod and staff keep me
   safe.

5 You prepare a banquet for me,
   where all my enemies can see me;
you welcome me by pouring ointment on
   my head
   and filling my cup to the brim.
6 Certainly your goodness and love will be
   with me as long as I live;
   and your house will be my home
   forever.

The Great King

24 The world and all that is in it belong
   to the Lord;
   the earth and all who live on it are his.
2 He built it on the deep waters beneath the
   earth
   and laid its foundations in the ocean
   depths.

3 Who has the right to go up the Lord's hill?
   Who is allowed to enter his holy temple?
4 He who is pure in act and in thought,
   who does not worship idols,
   or make false promises.
5 The Lord will bless him;
   God his Savior will declare him innocent.
6 Such are the people who come to God,
   who come into the presence of the God
   of Jacob.

7 Fling wide the gates,
    open the ancient doors,
    and the great king will come in!
8 Who is this great king?
  He is the Lord, strong and mighty,
    the Lord, victorious in battle!

9 Fling wide the gates,
    open the ancient doors,
    and the great king will come in!
10 Who is this great king?
   The Lord of armies, he is the great king!

A Prayer for Guidance and Protection

25   To you, Lord, I offer my prayer;
       2 in you, my God, I trust.
Save me from the shame of defeat;
    don't let my enemies gloat over me!
3 Defeat does not come to those who trust
     in you,
    but to those who are quick to rebel
     against you.

4 Teach me your ways, Lord,
    make them known to me.
5 Teach me to live according to your truth,
    because you are my Savior.
    All day long I trust in you.

6 Lord, remember your kindness and con-
     stant love,
    which you have shown from long ago.
7 Forgive the sins and errors of my youth.
  Because of your constant love and good-
     ness,
    remember me, Lord!

8 The Lord is righteous and good;
    he teaches sinners the way they should
     go.
9 He leads the humble in the right way

and teaches them his will.
¹⁰ In love and faithfulness he leads
all who obey his covenant and his commands.

¹¹ Keep your promise, Lord, and forgive my
sins,
because they are many.
¹² Those who obey the Lord
will learn from him the way they should
go.
¹³ They will always be prosperous,
and their children will live safely in the
land.
¹⁴ The Lord is the friend of those who obey
him,
and he teaches them his covenant.

¹⁵ I look to the Lord for help at all times,
and he rescues me from danger.
¹⁶ Turn to me, Lord, and be merciful to me,
because I am alone and weak.
¹⁷ Relieve me of all my worries
and save me from all my troubles.
¹⁸ Consider all my distress and suffering
and forgive all my sins.

¹⁹ Look at all the enemies I have;
see how much they hate me!
²⁰ Protect me and save me;
keep me from defeat,
because I come to you for protection.
²¹ May my goodness and honesty preserve
me,
because I trust in you.

²² From all their troubles,
save your people, God!

The Prayer of a Good Man

26 Declare that I am innocent, Lord,
    because I do what is right
and trust you completely.
2 Examine me and test me, Lord;
    judge my desires and thoughts.
3 Your constant love guides me;
    your faithfulness always leads me.

4 I do not keep company with worthless
    men;
    I have nothing to do with hypocrites.
5 I hate the company of evil men
    and avoid the wicked.

6 Lord, I wash my hands to show that I am
    innocent
    and march in worship around your al-
    tar.
7 I sing a hymn of thanksgiving
    and tell all your wonderful deeds.

8 Lord, I love the house where you live,
    the place where your glory dwells.
9 Do not destroy me with the sinners;
    spare me from the fate of murderers—
10 men who do evil at all times
    and are always ready to bribe.

11 As for me, I do what is right;
    be merciful to me and save me!

12 I am safe from all dangers;
    in public worship I praise the Lord!

A Prayer of Praise

27 The Lord is my light and my salva-
    tion;
    I will fear no one.

The Lord protects me from all danger;
  I will not be afraid.

2 When evil men attack me and try to kill
    me,
  they stumble and fall.
3 Even if a whole army surrounds me,
  I will not be afraid;
even if my enemies attack me,
  I will still trust God.

4 I have asked the Lord for one thing;
  one thing only do I want:
to live in the Lord's house all my life,
  to marvel at his goodness,
  and to ask his guidance there.

5 In times of trouble he will protect me in
    his shelter;
  he will keep me safe in his temple,
  and place me securely on a high rock.
6 So I will triumph over my enemies around
    me.
  With shouts of joy I will offer sacrifices
    in his temple;
  I will sing, I will praise the Lord!

7 Hear me, Lord, when I call to you!
  Be merciful and answer me!
8 "Come to me," you said.q
I will come to you, Lord;
9   don't hide yourself from me!

Don't be angry with me;
  don't turn your servant away.
You have been my help;
  don't leave me, don't abandon me,
  God, my Savior!

q"Come to me," you said; *Hebrew* I said to you, "Come to me" (*you
is singular,* Come *is plural*).

¹⁰ My father and mother may abandon me,
  but the Lord will take care of me.

¹¹ Teach me, Lord, what you want me to do
  and lead me along a safe path,
  because I have many enemies.
¹² Do not abandon me to my enemies,
  who attack me with lies and threats.

¹³ Certainly I will live to see
  the Lord's goodness to his people.
¹⁴ Trust in the Lord!
  Have faith, don't despair.
  Trust in the Lord!

A Prayer for Help

28 Lord, my defender, I call to you.
      Hear my cry!
  If you do not answer me,
    I will be among those who go down to
      the land of the dead.
² Hear me when I cry to you for help,
  with my hands lifted toward your holy
      temple.
³ Do not condemn me with the wicked,
  with those who do evil—
men whose words are friendly,
  but whose hearts are filled with hate.

⁴ Punish them for what they have done,
  for all the evil they have committed.
Punish them for all their deeds;
  give them what they deserve!
⁵ They take no notice of what the Lord has
      done,
  or of what he has made;
so he will punish them
  and destroy them forever.

⁶ Give praise to the Lord;
  he has heard my cry for help!

⁷ The Lord protects and defends me;
  I trust in him.
He has helped me, and so I am glad
  and sing hymns of praise to him.

⁸ The Lord protects his people;
  he defends and saves his chosen king.
⁹ Save your people, Lord,
  and bless those who are yours!
Be their shepherd,
  and take care of them forever.

The Voice of the Lord in the Storm

29 Praise the Lord, you gods;
      praise his glory and power.
² Praise the Lord's glorious name,
  bow down before the Holy One when
  he appears.

³ The Lord's voice is heard on the seas;
  the glorious God thunders,
  and his voice echoes over the ocean.
⁴ The Lord's voice is heard
  in all its might and majesty!

⁵ The Lord's voice breaks the cedars,
  even the cedars of Lebanon.
⁶ He causes the mountains of Lebanon to
  jump like calves,
  and Mount Hermon to leap like a young
  bull.

⁷ The Lord's voice makes the lightning
  flash.
⁸ His voice makes the desert shake;
  he shakes the desert of Kadesh.
⁹ The Lord's voice makes the deer give
  birth,
  and leaves the trees stripped bare,
  while in his temple all shout, "Glory to
  God!"

¹⁰ The Lord rules over the deep waters;
    he rules as king forever.
¹¹ The Lord gives strength to his people,
    and blesses them with peace.

A Prayer of Thanksgiving[r]

30   I praise you, Lord, because you have
        saved me
  and kept my enemies from gloating
    over me.
² I cried to you for help, Lord my God,
    and you healed me.
³ You brought me back from the world of
    the dead.
I was with those who go down to the
    depths below,
  but you restored my life.
⁴ Sing praise to the Lord,
    his faithful people!
Remember what the Holy One has done
  and give him thanks!
⁵ His anger lasts only a moment,
    his goodness for a lifetime.
There may be tears during the night,
    but joy comes in the morning.

⁶ I felt secure, and said to myself,
    "I will never be defeated."
⁷ You are good to me, Lord;
  you have kept me safe as in a mountain
    fortress.
But when you hid yourself from me,
    I was filled with fear.

⁸ I called to you, Lord;
    I begged for your help.
⁹ What good will come from my death?
  What profit from my going to the grave?
Are dead people able to praise you?
  Can they proclaim your unfailing good-
    ness?

[r]*Hebrew title:* A song for the dedication of the temple.

¹⁰ Hear me, Lord, and be merciful!
   Help me, Lord!

¹¹ You have changed my sadness into a joy-
      ful dance;
   you have taken off my clothes of
      mourning,
   and given me clothes of joy.
¹² So I will not be silent;
   I will sing praise to you.
Lord, you are my God,
   I will give thanks to you forever.

A Prayer of Trust in God

31   I come to you, Lord, for protection;
         never let me be defeated.
   You are a righteous God;
      save me, I pray!
² Hear me! Save me now!
   Be my refuge, to protect me;
      my defense, to save me.

³ You are my refuge and defense;
      guide me and lead me as you have
         promised.
⁴ Keep me safe from the trap that has been
         set for me;
      you are my shelter.
⁵ I place myself in your care.
   You will save me, Lord;
      you are a faithful God.

⁶ You hate those who worship false gods;
      but I trust in you.
⁷ I will be glad and rejoice,
      because of your constant love.
   You see my suffering;
      you know my trouble.
⁸ You have not let my enemies capture me;
      you have kept me safe.

⁹ Be merciful to me, Lord,
    because I am in trouble;
my eyes are tired from so much crying;
    I am completely worn out!
¹⁰ Sorrow has shortened my life,
    and weeping has reduced my years.
I am weak from all my troubles;ˢ
    even my bones are wasting away.

¹¹ All my enemies make fun of me;
    my neighbors scornᵗ me;
those who know me are afraid of me;
    when they see me in the street, they run
        away.
¹² I am forgotten by all, as though I had died;
    I am like something thrown away.
¹³ I hear many enemies whispering;
    terror is all around me!
They are making plans against me,
    plotting to kill me.

¹⁴ But my trust is in you, Lord;
    you are my God.
¹⁵ I am always in your care;
    save me from my enemies
    and from those who persecute me.
¹⁶ I am your servant;
    look on me with kindness;
    save me because of your constant love!
¹⁷ I call to you, Lord;
    don't let me be defeated!
May the wicked be defeated;
    may they be silent in the world of the
        dead.
¹⁸ Silence those liars—
    all the proud and arrogant,
    who speak with contempt about right-
        eous men!

¹⁹ How wonderful are the good things

ˢ*Some ancient translations* troubles; *Hebrew* iniquity. ᵗscorn; *Hebrew*
exceedingly.

you keep for those who fear you!
How wonderful is what you do in the sight
of everyone,
protecting those who trust you.
20 You hide them in the safety of your presence
from the plots of men;
in a safe shelter you hide them
from the insults of their enemies.

21 Praise the Lord!
How wonderfully he showed his love for
me,
when I was surrounded and attacked!
22 I was afraid, and thought
that you had thrown me out of your
presence.
But you heard my cry,
when I called to you for help.

23 Love the Lord, all his faithful people!
The Lord protects the faithful,
but harshly punishes the proud.
24 Be strong, be courageous,
all who hope in the Lord!

Confession and Forgiveness

32 Happy is the man whose sins are forgiven,
whose transgressions are pardoned.
2 Happy is the man whom the Lord does
not accuse of doing wrong,
who is free from all deceit.

3 When I did not confess my sins,
I was worn out from crying all day long.
4 Day and night you punished me, Lord;
my strength was completely drained,
as moisture is dried up by the summer
heat.

⁵ Then I confessed my sins to you;
  I did not conceal my wrongdoings.
. I decided to confess them to you,
    and you forgave all my transgressions.

⁶ So all your loyal people should pray to
    you in times of need;ᵘ
    when a great flood comes rushing, it will
      not reach them.
⁷ You are my hiding place;
    you will save me from trouble.
  I sing aloud of your salvation,
    because you protect me.

⁸ The Lord says, "I will teach you the way
    you should go;
  I will instruct you and advise you.
⁹ Don't be stupid like a horse or a mule,
    which must be controlled with a bit and
      bridle,
    to make it obey you."

¹⁰ The wicked will have to suffer,
    but those who trust in the Lord
    are protected by his constant love.
¹¹ All who are righteous, be glad and rejoice,
    because of what the Lord has done!
  All who obey him, shout for joy!

A Song of Praise

33 All you that are righteous,
      be glad because of what the Lord
        has done;
    praise him, all you that obey him!
² Give thanks to the Lord with the harp,
    sing to him with stringed instruments.
³ Sing a new song to him,
    play the harp with skill, and sing aloud!

ᵘ*Some ancient translations* need; *Hebrew* finding only.

⁴ The words of the Lord are true,
   and all his works are dependable.
⁵ The Lord loves what is righteous and just;
   his constant love fills the earth.

⁶ The Lord created the heavens by his com-
      mand,
   the sun, moon, and stars by his spoken
      word.
⁷ He gathered all the seas into one place;
   he shut up the ocean depths in store-
      rooms.

⁸ Fear the Lord, all the earth!
   Fear him, all peoples of the world!
⁹ When he spoke, the world was created;
   at his command everything appeared.

¹⁰ The Lord frustrates the purposes of the
      nations;
   he keeps them from carrying out their
      plans.
¹¹ But his plans endure forever,
   his purposes last eternally.
¹² Happy is the nation whose God is the
      Lord;
   happy are the people he has chosen for
      his own!

¹³ The Lord looks down from heaven
   and sees all mankind.
¹⁴ From where he rules he looks down
   on all who live on earth.
¹⁵ He forms all their thoughts,
   and knows everything they do.

¹⁶ A king does not win because of his power-
      ful army;
   a soldier does not triumph because of
      his strength.
¹⁷ War horses are useless for victory;
   their great strength cannot save.

¹⁸ The Lord watches over those who fear
            him,
        those who trust in his constant love.
¹⁹ He saves them from death;
        he keeps them alive in times of famine.

²⁰ We put our hope in the Lord;
        he is our helper and protector.
²¹ We are glad because of him;
        we trust in his holy name.

²² May your constant love be with us, Lord,
        as we put our hope in you.

In Praise of God's Goodness᷉

34   I will always thank the Lord;
            I will never stop praising him.
² I will praise him for what he has done;
        may all who are oppressed listen and be
            glad!
³ Proclaim with me the Lord's greatness;
        let us praise his name together!

⁴ I prayed to the Lord and he answered me;
        he freed me from all my fears.
⁵ The oppressed look to him and are glad;
        they will never be disappointed.
⁶ The helpless call to him, and he answers;
        he saves them from all their troubles.
⁷ His angel guards those who fear the Lord
        and rescues them from danger.

⁸ Find out for yourself how good the Lord
            is!
        Happy is the man who finds safety with
            him!
⁹ Fear the Lord, all his people;
        those who fear him have all they need.

᷉*Hebrew title:* David pretended to be crazy in the presence of
Abimelech, who sent him away; after leaving, David wrote this
psalm.

¹⁰ Even lions lack food and go hungry,
    but those who obey the Lord lack noth-
    ing good.

¹¹ Come, my young friends, and listen to me,
    and I will teach you to fear the Lord.
¹² Would you like to enjoy life?
    Do you want long life and happiness?
¹³ Then keep from speaking evil
    and from telling lies.
¹⁴ Turn away from evil and do good;
    desire peace and do your best to have it.

¹⁵ The Lord watches over the righteous
    and listens to their cries;
¹⁶ but he opposes those who do evil,
    so that even their own people forget
    them.
¹⁷ Righteous men call to the Lord and he
    listens;
    he rescues them from all their troubles.
¹⁸ The Lord is near to those who are dis-
    couraged;
    he saves those who have lost all hope.

¹⁹ The good man suffers many troubles,
    but the Lord saves him from them all;
²⁰ the Lord preserves him completely;
    not one of his bones is broken.
²¹ Evil will kill the wicked;
    those who hate the righteous will be
    punished.

²² The Lord will save his servants;
    those who go to him for protection will
    be spared.

A Prayer for Help

35 Oppose those who oppose me, Lord,
      and fight those who fight me!
² Take your shield and armor

and come to my help.
³ Lift up your spear and war ax
   against those who pursue me.
Tell me that you are my Savior!

⁴ May those who try to kill me
   be defeated and disgraced!
May those who plot against me
   be turned back and confused!
⁵ May they be like straw blown by the wind,
   as the angel of the Lord chases them!
⁶ May their path be dark and slippery,
   while the angel of the Lord strikes them
      down!

⁷ Without any reason they laid a trap for me
   and dug a deep hole to catch me.
⁸ But destruction will catch them before
      they know it;
   they will be caught in their own trap
   and fall into the hole they dug!ʷ

⁹ Then I will be glad because of the Lord;
   I will be happy because he saved me.
¹⁰ With all my heart I will say to the Lord,
   "There is no one like you!
You protect the weak from the strong,
   the poor and needy from the oppres-
      sor!"

¹¹ Evil men testify against me
   and accuse me of crimes I know nothing
      about.
¹² They pay me back evil for good,
   and I am full of despair.
¹³ But when they were sick, I dressed in
      mourning;
   I deprived myself of food;
   I prayed with my head bowed low,
¹⁴   as I would pray for a friend or a brother.

ʷ*One ancient translation* the hole they dug; *Hebrew* destruction.

I went around bent over in mourning,
   as one who mourns for his mother.

15 When I was in trouble, they were all glad
   and gathered around me to make fun of
     me;
strangers beat me
   and kept striking me.
16 They made me suffer, and made fun of me[x]
   glaring at me with hate.

17 How much longer, Lord, will you look on?
   Rescue me from their attacks;
   save my life from these lions!
18 Then I will thank you in the large assem-
    bly,
   I will praise you before a great crowd.

19 Don't let my enemies, those liars,
   gloat over my defeat!
Don't let those who hate me for no reason
   wink with delight over my sorrow!

20 They do not speak in a friendly way;
   instead they invent all kinds of lies
    about peace-loving people.
21 They accuse me, shouting,
   "We saw what you did!"
22 But you, Lord, have seen this.
   So don't be silent, Lord;
   don't keep yourself far away!
23 Wake up, Lord, and defend me;
   rise up, my God, and plead my cause.
24 You are righteous, Lord, so declare me
    innocent;
   do not let my enemies gloat over me,
    my God!
25 Do not let them say to themselves,
   "Well! Just what we wanted!"

---

[x]*One ancient translation* they made me suffer, and made fun of me;
Hebrew with the profane of mockers of a cake.

Do not let them say,
"We have defeated him!"

26 May those who gloat over my suffering
   be completely defeated and confused;
may those who claim to be better than I
   am
   be covered with shame and disgrace!

27 May those who are glad that I am acquit-
   ted
   shout with joy and say again and again,
"Great is the Lord;
   he is happy with the success of his servant!"
28 Then I will proclaim your righteousness,
   and I will praise you all day long.

The Wickedness of Man

36 Sin speaks to the wicked man
        deep in his heart;
   he rejects God, and does not fear him.
2 Because he has such a high opinion of
   himself,
   he thinks that God will not discover
   and condemn his sin.
3 His speech is evil and full of lies;
   he is no longer wise enough to do good.
4 He makes evil plans as he lies in bed;
   his conduct is not good,
   and he does not reject what is evil.

The Goodness of God

5 Lord, your constant love reaches the
   heavens,
   your faithfulness extends to the skies.
6 Your righteousness is firm like the great
   mountains,

your judgments are like the depths of
the sea.

You, Lord, care for men and animals.

7 How precious, God, is your constant love!
Men find protection under the shadow
of your wings.
8 They feast on the abundant food from
your house;
you give them to drink from the river of
your goodness.
9 You are the source of all life,
and because of your light we see the
light.

10 Continue to love those who know you
and to do good to those who are righteous.
11 Do not let proud men attack me
or wicked men make me run away.
12 See where evil men have fallen!
There they lie, unable to rise.

The Destiny of the Wicked and of the Good

37 Don't be worried on account of the
wicked;
don't be jealous of those who do wrong;
2 they will disappear like grass that dries up;
they will die like plants that wither.

3 Trust in the Lord and do good;
live in the land and be safe.
4 Seek your happiness with the Lord,
and he will give you what you most
desire.

5 Give yourself to the Lord;
trust in him, and he will help you;
6 he will cause your goodness to shine as the
light
and your righteousness as the noonday
sun.

7 Be calm before the Lord, and wait pa-
     tiently for him to act;
     don't be worried about those who pros-
        per
     or those who succeed in their evil plans.

8 Don't be angry; don't get mad!
     Don't be worried! It won't do you any
        good.
9 Those who trust in the Lord will live
     safely in the land,
     but the wicked will be driven out.

10 In just a little while, the wicked will
     disappear;
     you may look for them, but you will not
        find them;
11 but those who are gentle will live safely in
     the land
     and enjoy complete peace.

12 The wicked man plots against the good
     man
     and glares at him with hate.
13 The Lord laughs at the wicked man,
     because he knows that he will soon be
        destroyed.

14 The wicked draw their swords and bend
     their bows
     to kill the poor and needy,
     to slaughter men who are good;
15 but they will be stabbed by their own
     swords,
     and their bows will be smashed.

16 The little that a good man owns
     is worth more than the wealth of all the
        wicked;
17 because the Lord will take away the
     strength of the wicked,
     but protect those who are good.

¹⁸ The Lord takes care of those who obey
  him,
    and the land will be theirs forever.
¹⁹ They will not suffer when times are bad;
    they will have enough in time of famine.
²⁰ But the wicked will die;
      the enemies of the Lord will vanish like
        wild flowers;
      they will disappear like smoke.

²¹ The wicked man borrows, and doesn't pay
      back,
    but the good man is generous and lib-
      eral.
²² Those who are blessed by the Lord will
      live safely in the land,
      but those who are cursed by him will be
        driven out.

²³ The Lord guides a man safely in the way
      he should go
    and is pleased with his conduct.
²⁴ If he falls, he will not stay down,
    because the Lord will help him up.

²⁵ I am old now and no longer a boy,
      but I have never seen a good man aban-
        doned by the Lord,
      or his children begging for food.
²⁶ At all times he gives freely and lends to
      others,
    and his children are a blessing.

²⁷ Turn away from evil and do good,
    and you will live in the land forever;
²⁸ because the Lord loves what is right,
      and he does not abandon his faithful
        people.
  He protects them always,
    but the descendants of the wicked will
      be driven out.

²⁹ The righteous will live safely in the land
and possess it forever.

³⁰ The good man's words are wise,
and he speaks of what is right.
³¹ He keeps the law of his God in his heart
and never departs from it.

³² The wicked man watches the good man
and tries to kill him;
³³ but the Lord will not abandon him to his
enemy's power,
or let him be condemned when he is on
trial.

³⁴ Put your hope in the Lord and obey his
commandments;
he will give you the strength to possess
the land,
and you will see the wicked driven out.

³⁵ I have seen a wicked man who was a
tyrant;
he towered over everyone like a cedar
of Lebanon;ʸ
³⁶ but later Iᶻ passed by and he wasn't there;
I looked for him, but couldn't find him.

³⁷ Notice the good man, observe the righteous man;
a peaceful man has descendants;
³⁸ but sinners are completely destroyed,
and their descendants are wiped out.

³⁹ The Lord saves righteous men
and protects them in times of trouble.
⁴⁰ He helps them and rescues them;
he saves them from the wicked,
because they go to him for protection.

ʸ*One ancient translation* like a cedar of Lebanon; *Hebrew unclear.*
ᶻ*Some ancient translations* I; *Hebrew* he.

The Prayer of a Suffering Man

38 Lord, don't be angry and rebuke
          me!
     Don't punish me in your anger!
2 You have punished me and wounded me;
     you have struck me down.

3 Because of your anger, I am seriously ill;
     my whole body is diseased because of
        my sins.
4 I am drowning in the flood of my sins;
     I am weighted down by their heavy
        burden.

5 Because I have been foolish,
     my sores stink and rot.
6 I am bent over, I am crushed;
     I mourn all day long.
7 I am burning with fever,
     and I am seriously ill.
8 I am utterly crushed and defeated;
     my heart is troubled, and I groan with
        pain.

9 Lord, you know what I desire;
     you hear all my groans.
10 My heart is pounding, my strength is
        gone,
     and my eyes have lost their brightness.
11 My friends and neighbors will not come
        near me,
     because of my sores;
     even my family stays away from me.
12 Those who want to kill me lay traps for
        me,
     and those who want to hurt me threaten
        to ruin me;
     all day long they plot against me.

13 I am like a deaf man, and cannot hear,
     like a dumb man, and cannot speak;

14 I am like a man who does not answer,
    because he cannot hear.

15 I trust in you, Lord;
    and you, Lord my God, will answer me.
16 Don't let my enemies gloat over my dis-
        tress;
    don't let them boast about my downfall!
17 I am about to fall,
    and my pain is always with me.

18 I confess my sins,
    and they fill me with anxiety.
19 My enemies are healthy and strong;
    there are many who hate me for no
        reason.
20 Those who pay back evil for good
    are against me because I try to do right.

21 Do not abandon me, Lord,
    do not stay away, my God!
22 Help me now, Lord my Savior!

The Confession of a Suffering Man

39 I said, "I will be careful about
        what I do
    and not let my tongue make me sin;
    I will not say anything
        while evil men are near."
2 I kept quiet, not saying a word,
    not even about anything good!
    But my suffering only became worse,
3   and my heart was filled with anxiety.
    The more I thought, the more troubled I
        became;
    I could not keep from asking:
4 "Lord, how long will I live?
    When will I die?
    Teach me how soon my life may end."

5 How short you have made my life!
    In your sight my lifetime seems noth-
        ing.

Indeed every living man is no more than
    a puff of wind,
6 no more than a shadow!
All he does is for nothing;
    he gathers wealth, but doesn't know
      who will get it!

7 What, then, can I hope for, Lord?
    I put my hope in you.
8 Save me from all my sins
    and don't let fools make fun of me.
9 I will keep quiet, I will not say a word,
    because you made me suffer like this.
10 Don't punish me any more!
    I am about to die from your blows!
11 You punish a man's sins by your rebukes,
    and like a moth, you destroy what he
      loves.
Indeed a man is no more than a puff of
    wind!

12 Hear my prayer, Lord,
    and listen to my plea;
      don't be silent when I cry to you!
Like all my ancestors,
    I am only your guest for a little while.
13 Leave me alone so that I may have some
      happiness,
    before I go away and am no more.

A Song of Praise

40   I waited and waited for the Lord's
      help;
    then he listened to me and heard my
      cry.
2 He pulled me out of a dangerous pit,
    out of a muddy hole!
He set me safely on a rock
    and made me secure.
3 He taught me to sing a new song,

a song of praise to our God.
Many who see this will be afraid
      and will put their trust in the Lord.

⁴ Happy is the person who trusts the Lord,
      who does not turn to idols,
         or join those who worship false gods.
⁵ You have done many things for us, Lord
      my God;
         there is no one like you!
      You have made many wonderful plans
         for us.
   If I tried to speak of all of them,
      there would be more than I could tell.

⁶ You do not want sacrifices and offerings;
      you do not ask for animals burned
         whole on the altar,
         or sacrifices to take away sins.
   Instead, you have given me ears to hear
         you,
⁷   and so I answered, "Here I am;
      your instructions for me are in the book
         of the Law.
⁸ How I love to do your will, my God!
      I keep your teaching in my heart."

⁹ In the meeting of all your people, Lord,
      I told the good news that you save.
      You know that I will never stop telling
         it.
¹⁰ I have not kept the news of salvation to
         myself;
      I have always spoken of your faithful-
         ness and help.
   In the meeting of all your people I have
         not been silent
      about your constant love and loyalty.

¹¹ Lord, I know you will never stop being
         merciful to me!
      Your love and loyalty will always keep
         me safe.

A Prayer for Help
(Psalm 70)

¹² I am surrounded by many troubles—
  too many to count!
My sins have caught up with me,
  and I can no longer see;
they are more than the hairs on my head,
  and I have lost my courage.
¹³ Save me, Lord! Help me now!
¹⁴ May those who try to kill me
  be completely defeated and confused!
May those who are happy because of my
    troubles
  be turned back and disgraced!
¹⁵ May those who make fun of me
  be dismayed by their defeat!

¹⁶ May all who come to you
  be glad and joyful!
May all who love your salvation
  always say, "How great the Lord is!"

¹⁷ I am weak and helpless,
  but you, Lord, think of me.
You are my helper and Savior—
  do not delay, my God!

The Prayer of a Sick Man

41 Happy is the man who is concerned
      for the poor;
  the Lord will help him when he is in
    trouble.
² The Lord will protect him and preserve
    his life;
  he will make him happy in the land;
  he will not abandon him to the power of
    his enemies.
³ The Lord will help him when he is sick
  and restore him to health.

⁴ I said, "I have sinned against you, Lord;
    be merciful to me and cure me!"
⁵ My enemies say bad things about me.
    They say, "When will he die and be
        forgotten?"
⁶ Those who come to see me are not sin-
        cere;
    they gather all the bad news about me,
    and then go out and tell it everywhere.
⁷ All who hate me whisper to each other
        about me,
    they imagine the worst about me.
⁸ They say, "He is fatally ill
    and will never leave his bed again."
⁹ Even my best friend, the one I trusted
        most,
    the one who shared my food,
    has turned against me.

¹⁰ Be merciful to me, Lord, and restore my
        health;
    and I will pay my enemies back!
¹¹ I will know that you are pleased with me,
    because they will not triumph over me.
¹² You will help me, because I do what is
        right;
    you will keep me in your presence
        forever.

¹³ Let us praise the Lord, the God of Israel;
    praise him now and forever!
    Amen! Amen!

BOOK TWO
(Psalms 42—72)

The Prayer of a Man in Exile

42   As a deer longs for a stream of cool
            water,
    so I long for you, God.

2 I thirst for you, the living God;
    when can I go and worship in your
      presence?
3 Day and night I cry,
    and tears are my only food;
all the time my enemies ask me,
    "Where is your God?"

4 My heart breaks when I remember the
    past,
    when I went with the crowds to the
      house of God,
and led them as they walked along,
    a happy crowd, singing and shouting
      praise to God.
5 Why am I so sad?
    Why am I troubled?
I will put my hope in God,
    and once again I will praise him,
    my Savior and my God.

6 My heart is breaking,
    so I will remember him;
in my exile in the region of the Jordan,
    near Mount Hermon and Mount Mizar,
    I will remember him.
7 The ocean depths call out to each other,
    and the waterfalls of God are roaring!
They are like the waves of sorrow
    with which he floods my soul.
8 May the Lord show his constant love ev-
    ery day!
    May I sing praise to him every night,
    and pray to God, who gives me life.

9 To God, my defender, I say,
    "Why have you forgotten me?
Why must I go on suffering
    from the cruelty of my enemies?"
10 I am crushed by their insults,
    as they keep on asking me,
    "Where is your God?"

¹¹ Why am I so sad?
  Why am I troubled?
I will put my hope in God,
  and once again I will praise him,
  my Savior and my God.

The Prayer of a Man in Exile
(Continuation of Psalm 42)

43 God, declare me innocent,
      and defend my cause against the
        ungodly;
    deliver me from lying and evil men!
² You are my protector;
    why have you abandoned me?
  Why must I go on suffering
    from the cruelty of my enemies?

³ Send your light and your truth;
    may they lead me
    and bring me back to Zion, your sacred
      hill,
    and to your temple, where you live!
⁴ Then I will go to your altar, God,
    because you give me joy and happiness;
  I will play my harp and sing praise to you,
    God, my God!

⁵ Why am I so sad?
    Why am I troubled?
  I will put my hope in God,
    and once again I will praise him,
    my Savior and my God.

A Prayer for Protection

44 With our own ears we have heard it,
      God—
    our ancestors have told us about it,
  about the great things you did in their
      time,

in the days of long ago:
² how you yourself drove out the heathen,
    and established your people in their
    land;
how you punished the other nations,
    but caused your own to prosper.
³ Your people did not conquer the land
    with their swords;
they did not win it by their own power;
it was by your power and your strength,
    by the assurance of your presence,
    showing that you loved them.

⁴ You are my king and my God;
    you give*ᵃ* victory to your people.
⁵ By your power we defeat our enemies;
    by your presence we overcome our ad-
    versaries.
⁶ I do not trust in my bow,
    or trust in my sword to save me;
⁷ because you have saved us from our ene-
    mies,
    you have defeated those who hate us.
⁸ We will always praise you
    and give thanks to you forever.

⁹ But now, God, you have rejected us and
    let us be defeated;
    you no longer march out with our ar-
    mies.
¹⁰ You made us run away from our enemies,
    and they took for themselves what was
    ours.
¹¹ You allowed us to be slaughtered like
    sheep;
    you scattered us in foreign countries.
¹² You sold your own people for a small
    price,
    and made no profit from the sale.

ᵃSome ancient translations you give; *Hebrew* give!

¹³ Our neighbors see what you did to us,
    and they mock us and make fun of us.
¹⁴ You made us an object of contempt
        among the nations;
    they shake their heads at us in scorn.
¹⁵ I am always in disgrace,
    and I am covered with shame,
¹⁶ from hearing the sneers and insults
    of my enemies and adversaries.

¹⁷ All this has happened to us
        even though we have not forgotten you,
        or broken the covenant you made with
        us.
¹⁸ We have not been disloyal to you;
        we have not disobeyed your com-
        mands.
¹⁹ Yet you left us helpless among the wild
        animals;
    you abandoned us in deepest darkness.

²⁰ If we had stopped worshiping our God,
    and prayed to a foreign god,
²¹ you would surely have discovered it,
        because you know men's secret
        thoughts.
²² But it is for your sake that we are being
        killed all the time,
    that we are treated like sheep to be
        slaughtered.

²³ Wake up, Lord! Why are you asleep?
    Get up! Don't reject us forever!
²⁴ Why are you hiding from us?
    Don't forget our suffering and trouble!

²⁵ We fall crushed to the ground;
    we lie defeated in the dust.
²⁶ Get up and help us!
    Because of your constant love, save us!

A Royal Wedding Song

45 Beautiful words fill my mind,
as I compose this song for the
king;
my tongue is like the pen of a good
writer.

2 You are the most handsome of all men;
you are an eloquent speaker;
God has always blessed you!
3 Buckle on your sword, mighty king;
you are powerful and majestic!

4 Ride on in majesty to victory,
for the defense of truth and justice![b]
Your strength will win you great
victories!
5 Your arrows are sharp and pierce the
hearts of your enemies;
nations fall down at your feet.

6 The throne that God has given you
will last forever and ever!
You rule over your kingdom with justice;
7   you love what is right and hate what is
evil.
That is why God, your God, has chosen
you,
and has poured out more happiness on
you
than on anyone else.
8 The perfume of myrrh, aloes, and cassia is
on your clothes;
musicians entertain you in ivory pal-
aces.
9 Among the ladies of your court are daughters of kings,
and at the right of your throne stands
the queen,
wearing ornaments of finest gold.

[b]and justice; *Hebrew* and meekness of justice.

¹⁰ Bride of the king, listen to what I say—
    forget your people and your relatives.
¹¹ Your beauty will make the king desire
    you;
    he is your master, so you must obey
    him.
¹² The people of Tyre will bring you gifts;
    rich people will try to win your favor.

¹³ The princess is in the palace—how beauti-
    ful she is!
    Her gown is made of gold thread.
¹⁴ In her colorful gown she is led to the king,
    followed by her bridesmaids,
    and they also are brought to him.
¹⁵ With joy and gladness they come
    and enter the king's palace.

¹⁶ You, my king, will have many sons
    to take the place of your ancestors,
    and you will make them rulers over the
    whole earth.
¹⁷ My song will keep your fame alive
    forever,
    and everyone will praise you for all time
    to come.

God Is with Us

46 God is our shelter and strength,
    always ready to help in times of
    trouble.
² So we will not be afraid, even if the earth
    is shaken
    and mountains fall into the ocean
    depths;
³ even if the seas roar and rage,
    and the hills are shaken by the violence.

⁴ There is a river that brings joy to the city
    of God,
    to the sacred house of the Most High.

We will not be afraid

⁵ God lives in the city, and it will never be
   destroyed;
   at early dawn he will come to its help.
⁶ Nations are terrified, kingdoms are
   shaken;
   God roars out, and the earth dissolves.

⁷ The Lord Almighty is with us;
   the God of Jacob is our refuge!

⁸ Come, see what the Lord has done!
   See what amazing things he has done
   on earth!
⁹ He stops wars all over the world;
   he breaks bows, destroys spears,
   and sets shields on fire!
¹⁰ He says, "Stop your fighting, and know
   that I am God,
   supreme among the nations, supreme
   over the world!"

¹¹ The Lord Almighty is with us;
   the God of Jacob is our refuge!

Sing praise to God

The Supreme Ruler

47 Clap your hands for joy, all
      peoples!
    Praise God with loud songs!
[2] The Lord, the Most High, is to be feared;
    he is a great king, ruling over all the
      world.
[3] He gave us victory over the peoples;
    he made us rule over the nations.
[4] He chose for us the land where we live,
    the proud possession of his people,
      whom he loves.

[5] God goes up to his throne!
    There are shouts of joy and the blast of
      trumpets,
    as the Lord goes up!
[6] Sing praise to God;
    sing praise to our king!
[7] God is king over all the world;
    praise him with songs!

[8] God sits on his sacred throne;
    he rules over the nations.
[9] The rulers of the nations come together

with the people*c* of the God of Abraham.
The shields of all the warriors belong to
God;
he rules over all!

Zion, the City of God

48 The Lord is great, and must be
highly praised
in the city of our God, on his sacred
mountain.

2 Zion, the mountain of God, is high and
beautiful;
the city of the great king brings joy to
all the world!

3 God has shown that there is safety with
him
inside the fortresses of the city.

4 The kings gathered together
and came to attack Mount Zion.

5 When they saw it they were surprised;
they were afraid and ran away.

6 There they were seized with fear and anguish,
like a woman about to bear a child.

7 God destroys large ships with the east
wind.

8 We have heard about what God has done,
and now we have seen it
in the city of our God, the Lord Almighty;
he will keep the city safe forever.

9 Inside your temple, God,
we think of your constant love.

10 You are praised by people everywhere,
and your fame extends over all the
earth.

*c*With the people; *Hebrew* the people.

You rule with justice;
¹¹ let the people of Zion be glad!
You give right judgments;
    let there be joy in the cities of Judah!

¹² Walk all around Mount Zion and count its
        towers,
¹³   take notice of its walls, and examine its
        fortresses,
    so that you may tell the next generation
¹⁴   that this God is our God, forever and
        ever;
    he will lead us for all time to come.

The Foolishness of Trusting in Riches

49   Hear this, everyone!
        Listen, all people everywhere,
² great and small alike,
    rich and poor together.
³ I will think sensible thoughts;
    I will speak words of wisdom.
⁴ I will turn my attention to a riddle,
    and explain its meaning as I play the
        harp.

⁵ I am not afraid in times of danger,
    when I am surrounded by evil enemies,
⁶ by men who trust in their riches,
    who boast of their great wealth.
⁷ A man can never redeem himself;[d]
    he cannot pay God the price for his life,
⁸   because the payment for a man's life is
        too great.
What he can pay will never be enough
⁹   to keep him from the grave,
    to let him live forever.

¹⁰ He sees that even wise men die,
    as well as foolish and stupid men.

[d]*Some Hebrew manuscripts* himself; *other Hebrew manuscripts* his
brother.

They all leave their riches to their descendants.
11 Their graves*e* are their homes forever;
    there they stay for all time,
    even though they once had lands of
      their own.
12 A man's greatness cannot keep him from
      death;
    he will die like the animals.

13 See what happens to those who trust in
      themselves,
    the fate of those*f* who are satisfied with
      their wealth—
14 they are doomed to die like sheep,
    and death will be their shepherd.
  The righteous will triumph over them in
      the morning
    as their bodies decay in the land of the
      dead,
    far from their homes!*g*
15 But God will save me;
    he will take me from the power of
      death.

16 Don't be afraid when a man becomes rich,
    when his wealth grows even greater;
17 he cannot take it with him when he dies;
    his wealth will not go to the grave with
      him.
18 Even if a man is satisfied with this life,
    and is praised because he is successful,
19 he will join all his ancestors in death,
    where the darkness lasts forever.
20 A man's greatness cannot keep him from
      death;
    he will die like the animals.

*e*Some ancient translations* graves; *Hebrew* inner thoughts.   *f*One ancient translation* the fate of those; *Hebrew* after them.   *g*Hebrew unclear.

True Worship

50 The Almighty God, the Lord,
speaks;
he calls to the whole earth, from east to
west.
2 God shines from Zion,
the city perfect in its beauty.

3 Our God is coming, but not in silence;
a raging fire is in front of him,
a furious storm around him.
4 He calls heaven and earth as witnesses
to see him judge his people.
5 He says, "Gather my faithful people to
me,
those who made a covenant with me by
offering a sacrifice."
6 The heavens proclaim that God is righteous,
that he himself is judge!

7 "Listen, my people, and I will speak;
I will testify against you, Israel.
I am God, your God.
8 I do not reprimand you because of your
sacrifices
and the burnt offerings you always bring
me.
9 And yet, I do not need bulls from your
farms,
or goats from your flocks,
10 because the animals of the woods are mine
and the cattle on thousands of hills.
11 All the wild birds are mine
and all living things in the fields.

12 "If I were hungry I would not tell you,
because the world and everything in it
is mine.
13 Do I eat the flesh of bulls,
or drink the blood of goats?

The animals of the woods are mine

14 Let the giving of thanks be your sacrifice
to God,
and give the Almighty all the offerings
that you promised.
15 Call to me when trouble comes;
I will save you,
and you will praise me."

16 But God says to the wicked,
"Why should you recite my commandments?
Why should you talk about my covenant?
17 You refuse to let me correct you;
you reject my commands.
18 When you see a thief, you become his
friend,
and you associate with adulterers.

19 "You are always ready to speak evil;
you never hesitate to tell lies.
20 You are ready to accuse your own brothers,
and to find fault with them.
21 You have done all this, and I have said
nothing,
so you thought that I am like you.
But now I will reprimand you,
and make the matter plain to you.

22 "Listen to this, you that ignore me,
or I will destroy you;
and there will be no one to save you.
23 Giving thanks is the sacrifice that honors
me,
and I will surely save all who obey me."

A Prayer for Forgiveness*h*

51 Be merciful to me, God,
because of your constant love;

hHebrew, title: David wrote this psalm after the prophet Nathan had
spoken to him about his adultery with Bathsheba.

wipe away my sins,
because of your great mercy!
2 Wash away my evil,
and make me clean from my sin!

3 I recognize my faults;
I am always conscious of my sins.
4 I have sinned against you—only against
you,
and done what you consider evil.
So you are right in judging me;
you are justified in condemning me.
5 I have been evil from the time I was born;
from the day of my birth I have been
sinful.

6 A faithful heart is what you want;
fill my mind with your wisdom.
7 Remove my sin, and I will be clean;
wash me, and I will be whiter than
snow.
8 Let me hear the sounds of joy and gladness;
and though you have crushed and
broken me,
I will be happy once again.
9 Close your eyes to my sins,
and wipe out all my evil.

10 Create a pure heart in me, God,
and put a new and loyal spirit in me.
11 Do not banish me from your presence;
do not take your holy spirit away from
me.
12 Give me again the joy that comes from
your salvation,
and make my spirit obedient.
13 Then I will teach sinners your commands,
and they will turn back to you.

14 Spare my life, God my Savior,
and I will gladly proclaim your righteousness.

¹⁵ Help me to speak, Lord,
    and I will praise you.

¹⁶ You do not want sacrifices,
    or I would offer them;
  you are not pleased with burnt offerings.
¹⁷ My sacrifice is a submissive spirit, God;
    a submissive and obedient heart you
      will not reject.

¹⁸ God, be kind to Zion and help her;
    rebuild the walls of Jerusalem.
¹⁹ Then you will be pleased with the proper
    sacrifices,
    and with all burnt offerings;
    and bulls will be sacrificed on your altar.

God's Judgment and Grace[1]

52   Why do you boast, great man, of
        your evil?
    God's love is constant.
² You make plans to ruin others;
    your tongue is like a sharp razor.
    You are always inventing lies.
³ You love evil more than good
    and falsehood more than the truth.
⁴ You love to hurt people with your words,
    you liar!

⁵ So God will ruin you forever;
    he will take hold of you and pull you out
      of your tent;
    he will remove you from the land of the
      living.

---

[1]*Hebrew title:* David wrote this poem when Doeg, the Edomite, went
to Saul and told him that David had gone to the house of Abimelech.

⁶ Righteous people will see this and be
        afraid;
    they will laugh at you, and say,
⁷ "Look, here is a man who did not depend
        on God for safety,
    but instead trusted in his great wealth,
    and looked for security in being
        wicked!"

⁸ But I am like an olive tree growing near
        the house of God;
    I trust in his constant love forever and
        ever.
⁹ I will always thank you, God, for what
        you have done;
    in the company of your people
    I will proclaim that you are good.

The Wickedness of Men
(Psalm 14)

53 Fools say to themselves,
        "God doesn't matter."
    They are all corrupt,
        they have done terrible things;
        there is no one who does what is right.

² God looks down at men from heaven
        to see if there are any who are wise,
        any who worship him.
³ But they have all turned away,
        they are all equally bad;
    not one of them does what is right,
        not a single one.

⁴ "Don't they know?" God asks.
        "Are these evildoers ignorant?
    They live by robbing my people
        and do not pray to me."

5 But then they will become terrified,
   as they have never been before;
   because God scatters the bones of your
      enemies.
He will defeat them completely,
   because he has rejected them.

6 How I pray that salvation
   will come to Israel from Zion!
When God makes his people prosperous
      again,
   Jacob's descendants will be happy;
   the people of Israel will be glad.

A Prayer for Protection from Enemies*j*

54   Save me by your power, God;
      set me free by your might!
2 Hear my prayer, God;
   listen to my words!

3 Proud men are coming to attack me;
   cruel men are trying to kill me—
   men who do not care about God.

4 I know that God is my helper,
   that the Lord is my defender!
5 May God punish my enemies with their
      own evil!
He will destroy them because he is
      faithful.

6 Lord, I will gladly offer you a sacrifice;
   I will give you thanks,
   because you are good.
7 You have rescued me from all my
      troubles,
   and I have seen my enemies defeated.

j Hebrew title: David wrote this poem when the men of Ziph went to
Saul and told him that David was hiding in their territory.

A Prayer for Help

55 Hear my prayer, God;
don't turn away from my plea!
² Listen to me and answer me;
I am worn out by my worries.
³ I am upset by the threats of my enemies,
by oppression from the wicked.
They bring trouble on me;
they are angry with me and hate me.

⁴ Fear fills my heart,
and the terrors of death are heavy on
me.
⁵ I am gripped by fear and trembling;
I am overcome with horror.
⁶ I say, "I wish I had wings, like a dove!
I would fly away and find rest!
⁷ I would fly far away
and make my home in the desert.
⁸ I would hurry and find myself a shelter
from the raging wind and the storm."

I wish I had wings, like a dove!

⁹ Destroy them, Lord, and confuse their
speech,

because I see violence and riots in the
city.
10 Day and night they walk around the city
on its walls;
it is full of crime and trouble.
11 There is destruction everywhere;
the streets are filled with oppression
and fraud.

12 If it were an enemy making fun of me,
I could endure it;
if it were an opponent boasting over me,
I could hide myself from him.
13 But it is you, my companion,
my colleague and close friend!
14 We had intimate talks with each other,
and went with the crowd to the temple.
15 May death come suddenly upon my enemies;
may they go down alive into the land of
the dead!
Evil is in their homes and in their hearts.

16 But I call to the Lord God for help,
and he will save me.
17 My complaints and groans
go up to him morning, noon, and night,
and he will hear my voice.
18 He will bring me safely back
from the battles that I fight
against so many enemies.
19 God, who has ruled from eternity,
will hear me and defeat them;
there is nothing they can do about it,
because they do not fear him.

20 My former companion attacked his
friends;
he broke his promise.
21 His words were smoother than cream,
but there was hatred in his heart;
his words were as soothing as oil,
but they cut like sharp swords.

²² Leave your troubles with the Lord,
 and he will support you;
 he will never let a good man be defeated.

²³ But you, God, will throw those murderers
 and liars into the depths below,
 before half their life is over.
As for me, I will trust in you.

A Prayer of Trust in God^k

56 Be merciful to me, God,
 because I am being attacked;
 my enemies persecute me all the time!
² All day long my opponents attack me.
 There are so many who fight against
 me.
³ When I am afraid, O Most High,
 I put my trust in you.
⁴ I trust in God and praise his promise;
 in him I trust, and I will not be afraid.
 What can mere man do to me?

⁵ My enemies make trouble for me in ev-
 erything I do;
 they are always thinking about how to
 hurt me!
⁶ They gather in a hiding place
 and watch everything I do,
 hoping to kill me.
⁷ Punish^l them, God, for their evil;
 defeat these people in your anger!

⁸ You know how troubled I am;
 you have kept a record of my tears.
 Aren't they listed in your book?
⁹ The day I call to you,

^kHebrew title: This prayer was written by David after the Philistines
captured him in Gath.   ^lPunish; Hebrew Save.

my enemies will be turned back.
This I know—God is on my side!
[10] I trust in God and praise his promise;
I will praise the promise of the Lord.
[11] In him I trust, and I will not be afraid.
What can mere man do to me?

[12] God, I will offer you what I have promised;
I will give you my offering of praise,
[13] because you have rescued me from death
and kept me from defeat.
And so I walk in the presence of God,
in the light that shines on the living.

A Prayer for Help [m]

57   Be merciful to me, God, be merciful,
because I come to you for safety.
In the shadow of your wings I find protection,
until all danger is past.
[2] I call to God, the Most High,
to God, who supplies all my needs.
[3] He will answer from heaven and save me;
he will defeat my attackers.
God will show me his constant love and
faithfulness.

[4] I lie down among lions,
who are ready to devour men.
Their teeth are like spears and arrows;
their tongues are like sharp swords.

[5] God, show your greatness in the sky,
and your glory over all the earth!

[6] My enemies have spread a net to catch
me;
I am overcome with distress.

[m]*Hebrew title:* David wrote this psalm after he ran away from Saul
in the cave.

They dug a pit in my path,
  but fell into it themselves.

[7] I am ready, God;
  I am completely ready!
  I will sing and praise you!
[8] Wake up, my soul!
  Wake up, my harp and lyre!
  I will wake up the sun!
[9] I will thank you among the nations, Lord!
  I will praise you among the peoples!
[10] Your constant love reaches up to heaven,
  your faithfulness to the skies.
[11] God, show your greatness in the sky,
  and your glory over all the earth!

A Prayer for God to Punish the Wicked

58 Do you really give a just decision,
      you rulers?[n]
  Do you judge all men fairly?
[2] No! You think only of the evil you will do,
    and commit crimes of violence in the
    land.

[3] Evil men go wrong all their lives;
  they tell lies from the day they are born.
[4] They are full of poison, like snakes;
  they stop up their ears, like a deaf
    cobra,
[5] which does not hear the voice of the snake
    charmer,
  or the chant of the clever magician.

[6] Break their teeth, God;
  tear out the fangs of these fierce lions,
    Lord!
[7] May they disappear like water draining
    away;

[n]Hebrew unclear.

may they be crushed like weeds on the path.[o]
8 May they be like snails that dissolve into slime;
may they be like a baby born dead that never sees the light.
9 Before they know it, they are cut down like a bush;
in his fierce anger God will blow them away
while they are still living.[p]

10 The righteous will be glad when they see sinners punished;
they will wade through the blood of the wicked.
11 Men will say, "The righteous are indeed rewarded;
there is indeed a God who judges the world!"

A Prayer for Safety[q]

59 Save me from my enemies, my God;
protect me from those who attack me!
2 Save me from those evil men;
rescue me from those murderers!

3 Look! They are waiting to attack me;
cruel men are gathering against me.
It is not because of any sin or wrong I have done,
4 not because of any fault of mine, Lord,
that they hurry to their places.

5 Rise, Lord God Almighty, and come to my help;
see for yourself, God of Israel!

[o]*Hebrew unclear.* [p]*Verse 9 in Hebrew is unclear.* [q]*Hebrew title:* David wrote this psalm when Saul sent men to watch his house in order to kill him.

Wake up and punish the nations;
  show no mercy to those evil traitors!

6 They come back in the evening,
  snarling like dogs as they go about the
    city.
7 Listen to what they say!
Their tongues are like swords in their
    mouths,
  yet they ask, "Who will hear us?"

8 But you laugh at them, Lord;
  you make fun of all the nations!
9 My defender, I am protected by you;
  God, you are my refuge.
10 My God, who loves me, will come to me;
  he will let me see my enemies defeated.

11 Do not kill them, God, so that my people
    will not forget.
  Scatter them by your strength and de-
    stroy them,
  Lord, our protector!
12 Sin is on their lips; all their words are
    sinful;
  may they be caught in their pride!
Because they curse and lie,
13   destroy them in your anger;
  destroy them completely.
Then all people will know that God rules
    in Israel,
  that his rule extends over all the earth!

14 My enemies come back in the evening,
  snarling like dogs as they go about the
    city.
15 They roam around looking for food
  and complain if they do not get enough.

16 But I will sing about your strength;
  every morning I will sing aloud of your
    constant love.

You have been a refuge for me,
a shelter in my days of trouble.
17 I will praise you, my defender;
my refuge is God,
the God who loves me.

A Prayer for Deliverance*

60 You have rejected us, God, and defeated us;
you have been angry with us—but now
turn back to us!
2 You have made the land tremble, and you
have cut it open;
now heal its wounds because it is about
to fall apart!
3 You have made your people suffer much
trouble;
you have given us wine that made us
drunk.
4 You raised a banner for those who fear
you,
but they turned and ran from the
enemy.
5 Save us by your might; answer our prayer,
so that the people you love may be
rescued.

6 In his sanctuary God has said,
"In triumph I will divide Shechem,
and distribute Succoth Valley to my
people.
7 Gilead is mine, and Manasseh too;
Ephraim is my helmet,
and Judah my royal scepter.
8 But I will use Moab as my washbowl
and Edom as my sandal box.
Did Philistia think she would shout in
triumph over me?"

*Hebrew title: A psalm of David, for teaching, written when he was
fighting against the Arameans from Naharaim and from Zobah, and
Joab turned back and killed 12,000 Edomites in the Salt Valley.

⁹ Who will take me, God, into the fortified
    city?
  Who will bring me to Edom?
¹⁰ Have you really rejected us?
    Aren't you going to march out with our
      armies?
¹¹ Help us fight the enemy,
    because human help is worthless!
¹² With God on our side we will win;
    he will defeat our enemies.

Take me to a safe refuge

A Prayer for Protection

61   Hear my cry, God;
          listen to my prayer!
² In my despair, far from home,
    I call to you!

  Take me to a safe refuge,
³   because you are my protector,
      my strong defender against my ene-
        mies.

⁴ Let me live in your tent all my life;
    let me find safety under your wings.
⁵ You have heard my promises, God,
    and you have given me what belongs to
      those who honor you.

⁶ Add many years to the king's life;
    let him live on and on!
⁷ May he rule forever in your presence,
      God;
    protect him with your constant love
      and faithfulness.

⁸ So I will always sing praises to you,
    as I offer you daily what I have prom-
      ised.

Confidence in God's Protection

62   I depend on God alone;
        my salvation comes from him.
² He alone is my protector and Savior;
    he is my defender,
    and I shall never be defeated.

³ How much longer will all of you attack a
      man to defeat him,
    like a falling wall,
    like a broken-down fence?
⁴ You only want to bring him down from his
      place of honor;
    you take pleasure in lies.
  You speak words of blessing,
    but in your heart you curse him.

⁵ I depend on God alone;
    I put my hope in him.
⁶ He alone is my protector and Savior;
    he is my defender,
    and I shall never be defeated.
⁷ My salvation and honor depend on God;
    he is my strong protector;
    he is my shelter.

8 My people, trust in God at all times!
    Tell him all your troubles,
    because he is our refuge.

9 Men are like a puff of breath;
    mortal men are worthless.
  Put them on the scales and they weigh
      nothing;
    they are lighter than a mere breath.
10 Don't put your trust in violence;
    don't hope to gain anything by robbery;
  even if your riches increase,
    don't depend on them.

11 More than once I have heard God say
    that power belongs to him,
12   and that his love is constant.

  You yourself, Lord, reward every man
    according to his deeds.

Longing for God*s*

63   God, you are my God,
        and I long for you.
  My whole being desires you;
    my soul is thirsty for you,
    like a dry, worn-out, and waterless land.
2 Let me see you in the sanctuary;
    let me see how mighty and glorious you
      are.
3 Your constant love is better than life
      itself,
    and so I will praise you.
4 I will give thanks to you as long as I live;
    I will raise my hands to you in prayer.
5 My soul will feast, and be satisfied
    and I will sing glad songs of praise to
      you.

*s*Hebrew title: David wrote this psalm when he was in the desert of
Judea.

⁶ As I lie in bed I remember you;
    all night long I think of you,
⁷ because you have always been my help.
    In the shadow of your wings I sing for
      joy.
⁸ I cling to you,
    and your hand keeps me safe.

⁹ Those who are trying to kill me
    will go down into the land of the dead;
¹⁰ they will be killed in battle,
    and their bodies eaten by wolves.
¹¹ The king will rejoice because of God;
    all who make promises in God's name
      will be glad,
    but the mouths of liars will be shut.

A Prayer for Protection

64   I am in trouble, God—listen to my
        prayer!
    I am afraid—save me from my enemies!
² Protect me from the plots of the wicked,
    from mobs of evil men.
³ They sharpen their tongues like swords,
    and aim cruel words like arrows.
⁴ From ambush they shoot their arrows at
      good men;
    they shoot suddenly, and are not afraid.
⁵ They encourage each other in their evil
      plots;
    they talk about where they will place
      their traps.
    "No one must see them," they say.
⁶ They make evil plans, and say,
    "We have planned a perfect crime."
    The heart and mind of man are a mystery!

⁷ But God shoots his arrows at them,
    and suddenly they are wounded.

⁸ He will destroy them because of their
   words;ᵗ
   all who see them will shake their heads.
⁹ They will all be afraid;
   they will tell what God has done
   and think about his acts.
¹⁰ All righteous people will rejoice because
   of what the Lord has done;
   they will find safety in him;
   all good people will praise him.

Praise and Thanksgiving

65 God, people must praise you in Zion
   and give you what they have
   promised,
² because you answer prayers.
All men shall come to you
³ on account of their sins.
Our faults defeat us,ᵘ
   but you forgive them.
⁴ Happy are those whom you choose,
   whom you bring to live in your sanctuary!
We shall be satisfied with the good things
   of your house,
   the blessings of your sacred temple!

⁵ You answer us, God our Savior,
   and you save us by doing wonderful
   things.
People all over the world,
   and across the distant seas, trust in you.
⁶ You set the mountains in place by your
   strength,
   showing your mighty power.
⁷ You calm the roar of the seas
   and the noise of the waves;

ᵗHe will destroy them because of their words; *Hebrew* They will
destroy him, their words are against them.   *ᵘOne ancient translation* us; *Hebrew* me.

you calm the uproar of the peoples.
8 The whole world is afraid,
    because of the great things that you
      have done.
Your actions bring shouts of joy
    from one end of the earth to the other.

9 You show your care for the land by send-
      ing rain;
    you make it rich and fertile.
The streams you have given never run
      dry;
    they provide the earth with crops—
    this is what you have done.
10 You send abundant rain on the plowed
      fields
    and soak them with water;
you soften the soil with showers
    and cause the young plants to grow.
11 What a rich harvest your goodness pro-
      vides!
Wherever you go there is plenty!
12 The pastures are filled with flocks;
    the hillsides are full of joy.
13 The fields are covered with sheep;
    the valleys are full of wheat;
    they shout and sing for joy!

A Song of Praise and Thanksgiving

66 Praise God with shouts of joy, all
      people!
2 Sing to the glory of his name;
    offer him glorious praise!
3 Say to God, "How wonderful are the
      things you do!
Your power is so great
    that your enemies bow in fear before
      you.
4 Everyone on earth worships you;
    they sing praises to you,
    they sing praises to your name."

Sing to the glory of his name

⁵ Come and see what God has done,
    his wonderful acts among men.
⁶ He changed the sea into dry land;
    our ancestors crossed the river on foot.
  There we rejoiced because of what he had
    done.
⁷ He rules forever by his might
    and keeps his eyes on the nations.
  Let no rebels rise against him!

⁸ Praise our God, all nations;
    let your praise be heard.
⁹ He has kept us alive
    and has not allowed us to fall.
¹⁰ You have put us to the test, God;
    as silver is purified by fire,
    so you have tested us.
¹¹ You let us fall into a trap
    and placed heavy burdens on our backs.
¹² You let our enemies trample us;
    we went through fire and flood,
    but now you have brought us to a place
    of safety.ʸ

¹³ I will bring burnt offerings to your house;
    I will offer you what I promised.

ʸ*Some ancient translations* safety; *Hebrew* overflowing.

¹⁴ I will give you what I said I would,
　　when I was in trouble.
¹⁵ I will offer sheep to be burned on the altar;
　　there will be the aroma of burning
　　　goats;
　　I will sacrifice bulls and goats.

¹⁶ Come and listen, all who honor God,
　　and I will tell you what he has done for
　　　me.
¹⁷ I cried to him for help;
　　I was ready to praise him with songs.
¹⁸ If I had ignored my sins,
　　the Lord would not have listened to me.
¹⁹ But God has indeed heard me;
　　he has listened to my prayer.

²⁰ I praise God,
　　because he did not reject my prayer,
　　or keep back his constant love from me.

A Song of Thanksgiving

67　God, be merciful to us and bless us;
　　　look on us with kindness,
² that the whole world may know your will;
　　that all nations may know your salva-
　　　tion.

³ May the peoples praise you, God;
　　may all peoples praise you!

⁴ May the nations be glad and sing for joy,
　　because you judge the peoples with jus-
　　　tice
　　and guide all the nations.

⁵ May the peoples praise you, God;
　　may all peoples praise you!

⁶ The land has produced its harvest;

God, our God, has blessed us.
7 God has blessed us;
    may all people everywhere honor him.

A National Song of Triumph

68 May God rise up and scatter his
        enemies!
    May those who hate him run away from
        him!
2 As smoke is blown away, so he will drive
        them off;
    as wax melts in front of the fire,
    so will the wicked perish in God's pres-
        ence.
3 But the righteous will be glad and rejoice
        in his presence;
    they will be exceedingly happy.

4 Sing to God, sing praise to his name;
    prepare a way for him who rides on the
        clouds.
    His name is the Lord—be glad in his
        presence!

5 God, who lives in his sacred temple,
    cares for orphans and protects widows.
6 He gives the lonely a home to live in
    and leads prisoners out into happy free-
        dom;
    but rebels will live in a desolate land.

7 God, when you led your people,
    when you marched across the desert,
8 the earth shook, and the sky poured down
        rain,
    because of the coming of the God of
        Sinai,
    the coming of the God of Israel.
9 You caused abundant rain to fall,
    and restored your worn-out land;
10 your people made their home there;

in your goodness you provided for the
poor.

11 The Lord gave the command,
and many women carried the news:
12 "Kings and their armies are running
away!"
The women at home divided what was
captured;
13 they looked like doves covered with
silver,
whose wings glitter with fine gold.
(Why did some of you stay in the sheep
pens?)
14 When Almighty God scattered the kings
on Mount Zalmon,
he caused snow to fall there.

15 What a mighty mountain is Bashan,
a mountain of many peaks!
16 Why do you, from your mighty peaks,
look with scorn
on the mountain that God chose to live
on?
The Lord will live there forever!

17 With his many thousands of mighty chariots,
the Lord comes from Sinai[w] into the
holy place.
18 He goes up to the heights,
taking many captives with him;
he receives gifts from rebellious men.
The Lord God will live there.

19 Praise the Lord,
who carries our burdens day after day;
he is the God who saves us.
20 Our God is a God who saves;
he is the Lord, our Lord,
who rescues us from death.

[w]comes from Sinai; *Hebrew* in them, Sinai.

21 God will surely break the heads of his
        enemies,
      of those who persist in their sinful ways.
22 The Lord has said, "I will bring your
        enemies back from Bashan;
      I will bring them back from the depths
        of the ocean,
23 that you may wade*x* in their blood,
      and your dogs may lap up as much as
        they want."

24 God, your march of triumph is seen by all,
      the procession of God, my king, into his
        sanctuary.
25 The singers are in front, the musicians are
        behind,
      in between are the girls beating the tam-
        bourines.
28 "Praise God in the meeting of his people;
      praise the Lord, all the descendants of
        Israel!"
27 First comes Benjamin, the smallest tribe,
      then the leaders of Judah with their
        group,
      followed by the leaders of Zebulun and
        Naphtali.

28 Show your power, God,
      the power you have used on our behalf.
29 From your temple in Jerusalem,
      where kings bring gifts to you,
30 reprimand Egypt, that wild animal in the
        reeds;
      reprimand the nations, that herd of
        bulls with their calves,
      until they all bow down and offer you
        their silver.*y*
      Scatter those people who love to make
        war!

---

xSome ancient translations wade; *Hebrew* break.   *yThe Hebrew text is
unclear.*

[31] Ambassadors[z] will come from Egypt;
    the Ethiopians will raise their hands in
      prayer to God.

[32] Sing to God, kingdoms of the world,
    sing praise to the Lord,
[33] to him who rides in the sky,
    the ancient sky!
Listen to him shout with a mighty roar!
[34] Proclaim God's power;
    his majesty is over Israel,
    his might is in the skies.
[35] How wonderful is God in[a] his sanctu-
    ary,
    the God of Israel!
He gives strength and power to his people.

Praise God!

A Cry for Help

69 Save me, God!
    The water is up to my neck;
[2] I am sinking in deep mud,
    and there is no solid ground;
I am out in deep water,
    and the waves are about to drown me.
[3] I am worn out from calling for help,
    and my throat is aching;
my eyes are strained
    from looking for your help.

[4] Those who hate me for no reason
    are more numerous than the hairs on
      my head;
those who lie about why they are my
    enemies
    are strong and want to kill me.
They made me give up things I did not
    steal.

---

[z]*Some ancient translations* Ambassadors; *Hebrew unclear.* [a]*One ancient translation* in; *Hebrew* from.

5 My sins, God, are not hidden from you;
  you know how foolish I have been!
6 Don't let me bring shame to those who
    trust in you,
      Lord God Almighty!
  Don't let me bring disgrace to those who
      worship you,
        God of Israel!
7 It is for your sake that I have been in-
    sulted,
      and that I am covered with shame.
8 I am like a stranger to my brothers,
    like a foreigner to my family.

9 My devotion for your temple burns in me
    like a fire;
      the insults which are hurled at you fall
        on me.
10 I humble myself[b] by fasting,
    and people insult me;
11 I dress myself in clothes of mourning,
    and they make fun of me.
12 They talk about me in the streets,
    and drunkards make songs about me.

13 But as for me, I will pray to you, Lord;
    answer me, God, at a time you choose,
  because of your great love,
    because you keep your promise to save.
14 Save me from sinking in the mud;
    keep me safe from my enemies,
    and from the deep water.
15 Don't let the flood come over me;
    don't let me drown in the depths,
    or sink into the grave.

16 Answer me, Lord, in the goodness of your
    constant love;
      in your great compassion, turn to me!
17 Don't hide yourself from your servant;
    I am in great trouble—answer me now!

----

[b]*Some ancient translations* humble myself; *Hebrew* cry.

¹⁸ Come to me and save me;
    rescue me from my enemies.

¹⁹ You know how I am insulted,
    how I am disgraced and dishonored;
    you see all my enemies.
²⁰ Insults have broken my heart,
    and I am helpless.
  I had hoped for sympathy, but there was
      none;
    for comfort, but I found none.
²¹ When I was hungry, they gave me poison;
    when I was thirsty, they offered me
      vinegar.

²² May their feasts cause their ruin;
    may their celebrations*c* cause their
      downfall!
²³ Blind them so they cannot see;
    make their backs always weak!
²⁴ Pour out your anger on them;
    let your indignation overtake them!
²⁵ May their camps be left deserted;
    may no one be left alive in their tents!
²⁶ They persecute those whom you have
      punished;
    they talk about the sufferings of those
      you have wounded.
²⁷ Keep a record of all their sins;
    don't let them have any part in your
      salvation.
²⁸ May their names be erased from the book
    of the living;
    may they not be included in the list of
      your people.

²⁹ But I am needy and in pain;
    lift me up, God, and save me!

³⁰ I will praise God with a song;

---

c One ancient translation their celebrations; *Hebrew* those who are at peace.

I will proclaim his greatness by giving
  him thanks.
31 This will please the Lord more than offering him an ox,
    more than giving him a full-grown bull.
32 When the needy see this they will be glad;
    those who worship God will be en-
    couraged.
33 The Lord listens to those in need,
    and does not forget his people in prison.

34 Praise God, heaven and earth,
    the seas and all creatures in them!
35 He will save Zion,
    and rebuild the towns of Judah;
  his people will live there and possess the
    land;
36   the descendants of his servants will in-
    herit it,
    and those who love him will live there.

A Prayer for Help

(Psalm 40.13-17)

70 Save me, God!
    Lord, help me now!
2 May those who try to kill me
    be defeated and confused!
  May those who are happy because of my
    troubles
    be turned back and disgraced!
3 May those who make fun of me
    be dismayed by their defeat!

4 May all who come to you
    be glad and joyful!
  May all who love your salvation
    always say, "How great God is!"

5 I am weak and helpless;
    come quickly to me, God.

You are my helper and Savior—
     do not delay, Lord!

An Old Man's Prayer

71   Lord, I am safe with you;
          never let me be defeated!
2 Because you are righteous, help me and
     rescue me.
     Listen to me and save me!
3 Be my secure shelter,
     and a strong fortress[d] to protect me;
     you are my refuge and defense.

4 My God, rescue me from wicked men,
     from the power of cruel and evil men.
5 Lord, I put my hope in you;
     I have trusted in you since I was young.
6 I have relied on you all my life;
     you have protected[e] me since I was
          born;
     I will always praise you!

7 My life has been a mystery to many,
     but you are my strong defender.
8 All day long I praise you
     and proclaim your glory.
9 Do not reject me now that I am old;
     do not abandon me now that I am fee-
          ble!
10 My enemies want to kill me;
     they talk and plot against me.
11 They say, "God has abandoned him;
     let us go after him and catch him,
     because there is no one to rescue him!"

12 Don't stay so far away, God;
     my God, help me now!
13 May those who attack me
     be defeated and destroyed!

[d]One ancient translation a strong fortress; Hebrew to go always you
commanded. [e]Some ancient translations protected; Hebrew unclear.

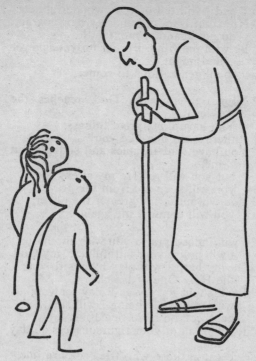

I am old and my hair is gray

May those who try to hurt me
   be shamed and disgraced!
¹⁴ I will always put my hope in you;
   I will praise you more and more.
¹⁵ I will tell of your righteousness;
   all day long I will speak of your salva-
      tion,
   though it is more than I can understand.
¹⁶ I will praise your power, Lord God;
   I will proclaim your righteousness,
      yours alone.

¹⁷ You have taught me ever since I was
      young,

and I still tell of your wonderful acts.
18 Now that I am old and my hair is gray,
    do not abandon me, God!
Be with me while I proclaim your power
    and might
    to all generations to come.

19 Your righteousness, God, reaches the
    skies.
    You have done great things;
    there is no one like you!
20 You have sent troubles and suffering on
    me,
    but you will restore my strength;
    you will keep me from the grave.
21 You will make me greater than ever;
    you will comfort me again.

22 I will indeed praise you with the harp;
    I will praise your faithfulness, my God.
On my harp I will play hymns to you,
    the Holy One of Israel.
23 I will shout for joy as I play for you;
    with my whole being I will sing,
    because you have saved me.
24 I will speak of your righteousness all day
    long,
    because those who tried to harm me
    have been defeated and disgraced.

A Prayer for the King

72 Teach the king to judge with your
    righteousness, God,
    share with him your own justice,
2 so that he will rule over your people with
    justice,
    and govern the poor with righteousness.
3 May the land enjoy prosperity;
    may it experience righteousness.
4 May the king judge the poor fairly;
    may he help the needy

and defeat the oppressors!
5 May your people worship you as long as
the sun shines,
as long as the moon gives light, for all
time.

6 May the king be like rain on the fields,
like showers falling on the land.
7 May righteousness flourish in his lifetime,
and prosperity last as long as the moon
shines.

8 His kingdom will reach from sea to sea,
from the Euphrates River to the ends of
the earth.
9 The peoples of the desert will bow down
before him;
his enemies will lie flat in the dust.
10 The kings of Spain and of the islands will
offer him gifts;
the kings of Arabia and Ethíopia will
bring him offerings.
11 All the kings will bow down before him;
all nations will serve him!

12 He rescues the poor who call to him,
and those who are needy and neglected.
13 He has pity on the weak and poor;
he saves the lives of those in need.
14 He rescues them from oppression and violence;
their lives are precious to him.

15 Long live the king!
May he be given gold from Arabia;
may prayers be said for him at all times;
may God's blessings be on him always!
16 May there be plenty of grain in the land;
may the hills be covered with crops,
as fruitful as those of Lebanon.
May the cities be filled with people,
like grass growing in the fields.

¹⁷ May his name never be forgotten;
       may his fame last as long as the sun.
    May all nations praise him,
       may all people ask God to bless them
          as he has blessed the king.

¹⁸ Praise the Lord, the God of Israel,
       who alone does these wonderful things!
¹⁹ Praise his glorious name forever,
       and may his glory fill the whole earth!
       Amen! Amen!

²⁰ The end of the prayers of David, the son
       of Jesse.

BOOK THREE
(Psalms 73–89)

The Justice of God

73   God is indeed good to Israel,
          to those who have pure hearts!
² But I was about to fall down;
       my feet were about to slip,
³ because I was jealous of the proud,
       and I saw that the wicked are rich.

⁴ They do not suffer pain;
       they are strong and healthy.
⁵ They don't suffer as other men do;
       they don't have the troubles that others
          have.
⁶ And so they wear pride like a necklace,
       and violence like a robe;
⁷ their hearts pour out evil,ᶠ
       and their minds are filled with wicked
          schemes.
⁸ They make fun of others and speak of evil
       things;

ᶠ*Some ancient translations* their hearts pour out evil; *Hebrew un-*
clear.

they are proud and talk about oppress-
ing others.
9 They speak evil of God in heaven,
   and give arrogant orders to men on
   earth,
10 so that even God's people turn to them
   and eagerly believe all they say.g
11 They say, "God will not know;
   the Most High will not find out!"
12 This is what the wicked are like.
   They have plenty and are always getting more.
13 Is it for nothing, then, that I have kept
   myself pure,
   and my hands clean from sin?
14 God, you have made me suffer all day
   long;
   every morning you have punished me!

15 If I had said such things,
   I would have been untrue to your people.
16 So I tried hard to understand this,
   even though it was so difficult,
17 until I went into your temple
   and understood what will happen to the
   wicked.

18 Surely you put them in slippery places
   and make them fall to destruction!
19 They are instantly destroyed;
   they go down to a horrible end!
20 Lord, they are like a dream that goes away
   in the morning;
   when you wake up you forget what they
   were like.

21 When my thoughts were bitter,
   and my feelings were hurt,
22 I was stupid, and did not understand;
   I acted like an animal toward you.

gHebrew unclear.

²³ Yet I am always with you,
   and you hold me by the hand.
²⁴ You guide me with your advice,
   and at the end you will receive me with
      honor.
²⁵ What else do I have in heaven but you?
   since I have you, what else do I want on
      earth?
²⁶ My mind and my body may grow weak,
   but God is my strength;
   he is all I ever want!

²⁷ Surely those who abandon you will die,
   and you will destroy those who are un-
      faithful to you.
²⁸ But as for me, how wonderful to be near
      God!
   In the Lord God I find protection,
   to proclaim all that he has done.

A Prayer for National Deliverance

74   Why have you abandoned us like
      this, God?
   Will you be angry with your own people
      forever?
² Remember your people, whom you chose
      to be yours a long time ago,
   the people you redeemed to be your
      own tribe.
   Remember Mount Zion, where you
      have lived!
³ Come and walk over these total ruins;
   our enemies have destroyed everything
      in the temple!

⁴ Your enemies shout in triumph in your
      meeting place;
   they have taken over the temple.
⁵ They looked like woodsmen
   cutting down trees with their axes.
⁶ They smashed all the wooden panels

with their axes and battering rams.
.⁷ They set your temple on fire;
  they profaned the place where you are
    worshiped;
  they wrecked it all.
⁸ They decided to crush us completely;
  they burned down every holy place in
    the land.

⁹ All our sacred symbols are gone;
  there are no prophets left,
  and no one knows how long this will
    last.
¹⁰ How long, God, will our enemies make
    fun of us?
  Will they insult your name forever?
¹¹ Why have you refused to help us?
  Why do you keep your hands behind
    you?ʰ

¹² But God, you have been our king from the
    beginning;
  you win victories on earth.
¹³ With your mighty strength you divided
    the sea
  and smashed heads of the sea mon-
    sters;
¹⁴ you crushed the heads of the monster
    Leviathan,
  and gave the desert people his dead
    body to eat.
¹⁵ You made springs and fountains flow;
  you dried up large rivers.
¹⁶ You created the day and the night;
  you set the sun and the moon in their
    places;
¹⁷ you set the limits of the earth;
  you made summer and winter.

¹⁸ But remember, Lord, that your enemies
    make fun of you;

ʰWhy do you keep your hands behind you; Hebrew unclear.

that they are foolish and despise you.
19 Don't abandon your helpless people to
    their cruel enemies;
    don't forget your persecuted people!

20 Remember the covenant you made with
    us.
    There is violence in every dark corner
    of the land!
21 Don't let the oppressed be defeated,
    but let the poor and needy praise you.

22 Rise, God, and defend your cause!
    Remember that the godless make fun of
    you all day long!
23 Don't forget the angry shouts of your ene-
    mies,
    the continuous noise made by your
    foes.

God the Judge

75 We praise you, God, we praise you!
    We proclaim how great you are,
    and tell*i* the wonderful things you have
    done!

2 "I have set a time for judgment," says
    God,
    "and I will judge with fairness.
3 Though the earth and all who live on it
    disappear,
    I will keep its foundations firm.
4 I tell the proud not to brag,
    and the wicked not to be arrogant;
5 I tell them to quit showing off,
    and to stop their bragging."

6 Judgment does not come from the east or
    from the west,

iSome ancient translations We proclaim how great you are, and tell;
Hebrew Your name is near and they tell.

from the north or from the south;*j*
⁷ it is God who does the judging,
   putting some down and lifting others
   up.
⁸ The Lord holds a cup in his hand,
   full of fresh wine, very strong;
 he pours it out, and all the wicked drink
   it;
 . they drink it down to the last drop.

⁹ But I will never stop speaking of the God
   of Jacob,
   or singing praises to him.
¹⁰ He will break the power of the wicked,
   but the power of the righteous will be
   increased.

God the Victor

76 God is well known in Judah,
       and famous in Israel.
² He has his home in Jerusalem;
   he lives on Mount Zion.
³ There he broke the arrows of the enemies,
   their shields and swords, yes, all their
   weapons.

⁴ How glorious you are, God!
   How majestic; as you return from the
   mountains
 · where you defeated your foes!
⁵ Their brave soldiers have been stripped of
   . their loot,
   and are now sleeping the sleep of death;
   there is no one left to use their weapons.
⁶ When you threatened . them, God of
   Jacob,
   the horses and their riders fell dead.

⁷ But you—how men fear you!

---

*j*from the north or from the south; *Hebrew* from the mountains of the
south.

Who can stand in your presence
when you are angry?
8 You made your judgment known from
heaven;
the earth was afraid and lay still,
9 when you rose up to pronounce judgment,
to save all the oppressed on earth.

10 Men's anger only results in more praise
for you;
those who survive the wars will keep
your festivals.*k*
11 Give the Lord your God what you promised him;
all you nearby nations bring gifts to
him.
God makes men fear him;
12 he humiliates proud princes,
and terrorizes great kings.

Comfort in Time of Distress

77 I cry aloud to God;
I cry aloud, and he hears me.
2 In time of trouble I pray to the Lord;
all night long I lift my hands in prayer,
but I cannot find comfort.
3 I think of God, and I sigh;
I meditate, and I feel discouraged.

4 He doesn't let me sleep;
I am so worried that I cannot speak.
5 I think of days gone by
and remember years of long ago.
6 I spend the night in deep thought;*l*
I meditate, and this is what I ask myself:

7 "Will the Lord always reject me?
Will he never again be pleased with me?

k One ancient translation will keep your festivals; *Hebrew unclear.*
l Some ancient translations deep thought; *Hebrew song.*

⁸ Has he stopped loving me?
    Is his promise no longer good?
⁹ Has God forgotten to be merciful?
    Has anger taken the place of his com-
       passion?"
¹⁰ Then I said, "What hurts me most is
       this—
    that God is no longer powerful."

¹¹ I will remember your great acts, Lord;
    I will recall the wonders you did in the
       past.
¹² I will think about all that you have done;
    I will meditate on all your deeds.

¹³ Everything you do, God, is holy!
    No god is as great as you!
¹⁴ You are the God who works miracles;
    you showed your might among the na-
       tions.
¹⁵ By your power you saved your people,
    the descendants of Jacob and of Joseph.

¹⁶ When the waters saw you, God, they were
       afraid,
    and the depths of the sea trembled.
¹⁷ The clouds poured down rain;
    thunder crashed from the sky,
    and lightning flashed in all directions.
¹⁸ The crash of your thunder rolled out,
    and flashes of lightning lit up the whole
       world;
    the earth trembled and shook.
¹⁹ You walked through the sea;
    you crossed the deep ocean,
    but your footprints could not be seen.
²⁰ You led your people like a shepherd,
    with Moses and Aaron in charge of
       them.

God and His People

78 Listen, my people, to my teaching,
and pay attention to what I say.
2 I am going to speak to you,
and tell you mysteries from the past,
3 things we have heard and known,
that our ancestors have told us.
4 We will not keep them from our children,
but will tell the next generation
about the Lord's power and his mighty
acts,
and the wonderful things that he has
done.

5 He gave laws to the people of Israel,
and commandments to the descendants
of Jacob.
He gave orders to our ancestors
to teach his laws to their children,
6 so that the next generation might learn
them,
and in turn should tell their children.
7 In this way they also would put their trust
in God,
and not forget what he had done,
but always obey his commandments.
8 They should not be like their ancestors,
a rebellious and disobedient people,
whose trust in God was never firm,
and who did not remain faithful to him.

9 The Ephraimites, who fought with bows
and arrows,
ran away on the day of battle.
10 They did not keep their covenant with
God;
they refused to obey his law.
11 They forgot what he had done,
the miracles that he had shown them.
12 While their ancestors watched, God performed a miracle

in the field of Zoan, in the land of
Egypt.
13 He divided the sea and led them through;
he made the waters stand like walls.
14 By day he led them with a cloud,
and all night long with the light of a fire.
15 He split rocks open in the desert,
and gave them water from the depths.
16 He caused a stream to come out of the
rock,
and made the water flow like a river.

17 But they continued to sin against God,
and rebelled in the desert against the
Most High.
18 They deliberately put God to the test,
by demanding the food they wanted.
19 They spoke against God, saying,
"Can God set a table in the desert?
20 It is true that he struck the rock,
and water flowed out in a torrent;
but can he also provide us with bread,
and give his people meat?"

21 And so the Lord was angry when he heard
them;
he attacked his people with fire,
and his anger against them grew,
22 because they had no faith in him,
and didn't believe that he would save
them.
23 But he spoke to the sky above,
and commanded its doors to open;
24 he gave them grain from heaven,
by sending down manna for them to
eat.
25 So they ate the food of angels.
God gave them all they could eat.
26 Then he caused the east wind to blow,
and by his power he stirred up the south
wind,
27 and sent down birds on them as thick as
dust,

as many as the grains of sand on the
shore;
28 they fell in the middle of the camp,
all around the tents.
29 So the people ate and were satisfied;
God gave them all they wanted.
30 But while they were still eating,
even before they had satisfied themselves,
31 God became angry with them,
and killed the strongest men,
the best young men of Israel!

32 In spite of all his miracles the people kept
on sinning,
and would not believe;
33 so he ended their days like a breath,
their lives with sudden disaster.
34 But when he would kill some of them,
the rest would turn to him;
they would repent and pray earnestly to
him.
35 They remembered that God was their
protector,
that the Most High was their Savior.
36 But their words were all lies,
and everything they said was flattery.
37 They were not loyal to him;
they were not faithful to their covenant
with him.

38 But God was merciful to his people.
He forgave their sin
and did not destroy them.
Many times he kept from being angry
and restrained his fury.
39 He remembered that they were only men,
and like a wind that blows by and is
gone.

40 How often they rebelled against him in
the desert;

how many times they made him sad!
41 Again and again they put God to the test,
   and made the Holy One of Israel angry.
42 They forgot his great power;
   they forgot the time he saved them
   from their enemies,
43 and performed his mighty acts and miracles
   in the field of Zoan, in the land of
   Egypt.
44 He turned the rivers into blood,
   so that the Egyptians couldn't drink
   from their streams.
45 He sent flies among them, that tormented
   them,
   and frogs, that ruined their fields.
46 He sent caterpillars to eat their crops,
   and grasshoppers to destroy their fields.
47 He killed their grapevines with hail,
   and their fig trees with frost.
48 He killed their cattle with hail,
   and their flocks with lightning.
49 He blasted them with his furious anger
   and fierce rage;
   he caused them great distress
   by sending the destroying angels.
50 He did not restrain his anger,
   or spare their lives,
   but killed them with a plague.
51 He killed the firstborn sons
   of all the families in Egypt.

52 Then he led his people out like a shepherd;
   he guided them through the desert.
53 He led them safely, and they were not
   afraid;
   but the sea covered their enemies.
54 He brought them to his holy land,
   to the mountains which he himself con-
   quered.
55 He drove out the inhabitants as his people
   advanced;

he divided the land among the tribes of
    Israel,
and there let them settle in their tents.

⁵⁶ But they rebelled against Almighty God,
    and put him to the test.
They did not obey his commandments,
⁵⁷   but were rebellious and disloyal like
        their ancestors,
    unreliable as arrows shot from a
        crooked bow.
⁵⁸ They angered him with their heathen
        places of worship,
    and made him jealous with their idols.
⁵⁹ God was angry when he saw it,
    and so rejected his people completely.
⁶⁰ He abandoned his tent in Shiloh,
    the home where he had lived among
        men.
⁶¹ He allowed the enemies to capture the
        covenant box,
    where his power and glory were seen.
⁶² He was angry with his own people,
    and let them be killed by their enemies.
⁶³ Young men were killed in war,
    and young women had no one to marry.
⁶⁴ Priests were killed by swords,
    and their widows could not mourn for
        them.

⁶⁵ At last the Lord woke up as though from
        sleep;
    he was like a strong man excited by
        wine.
⁶⁶ He drove his enemies back,
    in lasting and shameful defeat.
⁶⁷ He rejected the descendants of Joseph;
    he did not select the tribe of Ephraim.
⁶⁸ Instead he chose the tribe of Judah,
    and Mount Zion, which he dearly loves.
⁶⁹ There he built his temple,
    like his home in heaven;

he made it firm like the earth,
  secure for all time.

70 He chose his servant David;
    he took him from taking care of the
      sheep
71   and looking after the lambs.
  He made him king of Israel,
    the shepherd of the people of God.
72 David took care of them with complete
      devotion
    and led them with skill.

A Prayer for the Nation's Deliverance

79   God, the heathen have invaded your
      people's land!
    They have profaned your holy temple
  and left Jerusalem in ruins.
2 They left the bodies of your people for
    birds to eat,
    the bodies of your servants for wild
      animals.
3 They shed your people's blood like water;
    blood flowed like water all over Jeru-
      salem,
    and no one was left to bury the corpses.
4 The nations around us make fun of us;
    they laugh at us and mock us.

5 How long will you be angry with us, Lord?
    Forever?
  Will your anger continue to burn like
    fire?
6 Be angry with the nations that do not wor-
    ship you,
    with the people who reject you!
7 They have killed our people
  and ruined our country.

8 Do not punish us for the sins of our ances-
      tors,

but have mercy on us now,
    because we have lost all hope.
⁹ Help us, God our Savior,
    for the sake of your own honor;
rescue us and forgive our sins,
    so that people will praise you.
¹⁰ Why should the nations ask us,
    "Where is your God?"
Let us see you punish the nations
    for shedding the blood of your servants!

¹¹ Listen to the groans of the prisoners,
    and by your great power free those who
    are condemned to die.
¹² Lord, pay the other nations back seven
    times,
    for all the insults they have hurled at
    you.
¹³ And we, your people, the sheep of your
    flock,
    will thank you forever
    and praise you for all time to come.

A Prayer for the Nation's Restoration

80 Listen to us, Shepherd of Israel;
    hear us, leader of your flock.
Seated on your throne on the cherubim,
²   reveal your love for the tribes of
    Ephraim, Benjamin, and Manasseh!
Show us your strength;
    come and save us!

³ Bring us back, God!
    Show us your love, and we will be
    saved!

⁴ How much longer, Lord God Almighty,
    will you be angry with your people's
    prayers?
⁵ You have given us tears to eat,
    a large cup of tears to drink.

⁶ You let the neighboring nations fight over
   our land,
       and our enemies make fun of us.

⁷ Bring us back, Almighty God!
       Show us your love, and we will be
       saved!

⁸ You brought a grapevine out of Egypt;
       you drove out other nations and
       planted it in their land.
⁹ You cleared a place for it to grow;
       its roots went deep, and it spread out
       over the whole land.
¹⁰ It covered the hills with its shade,
       the giant cedars with its branches.
¹¹ It extended its branches to the Mediterranean Sea,
       and as far as the Euphrates River.
¹² Why did you break down the fences
   around it?
       Now anyone passing by can steal its
       grapes;
¹³   wild pigs trample it down,
       and all the wild animals eat it.

¹⁴ Turn to us, Almighty God!
       Look down from heaven at us;
       come and save your grapevine!
¹⁵ Come and save this vine that you yourself
   planted,
       this young vine you made grow so
       strong!

¹⁶ Our enemies have set it on fire and cut it
   down;
       look at them in anger and destroy them!
¹⁷ Protect and preserve the people you have
   chosen,
       the nation you made grow so strong!
¹⁸ We will never turn away from you again;
       keep us alive, and we will praise you.

¹⁹ Bring us back, Lord God Almighty!
   Show us your love, and we will be
      saved!

A Song for a Festival

81 Shout with joy to God our defender;
      sing praises to the God of Jacob!
² Start the music and play the tambourines;
   play pleasant music on the harps and
      the lyres.
³ Blow the horn for the festival;
   when the moon is new, and when the
      moon is full.
⁴ This is the law in Israel,
   an order from the God of Jacob.
⁵ He commanded it to the people of Israel,
   when he marched out against the land
      of Egypt.

I hear an unfamiliar voice saying,
⁶ "I took the heavy loads off your backs;
   I let you put down your workbaskets.
⁷ When you were in trouble you called to
      me, and I saved you.
   From my hiding place in the storm, I
      answered you;
   I put you to the test at the springs of
      Meribah.

⁸ "Listen, my people, to my warning;
   Israel, how I wish you would listen to
      me!
⁹ You must never serve a foreign god,
   or worship anyone else but me.
¹⁰ I am the Lord, your God,
   who brought you out of the land of
      Egypt.
   Open your mouth, and I will feed you.

¹¹ "But my people would not listen to me;

Israel would not obey me.
¹² So I let them go their stubborn ways
and do whatever they wanted.
¹³ How I wish my people would listen to me;
how I wish they would obey me!
¹⁴ I would quickly defeat their enemies
and conquer all their foes.
¹⁵ Those who hate me would bow in fear
before me;
their punishment would last forever.
¹⁶ I would feed you with the finest wheat
and satisfy you with wild honey."

God the Supreme Ruler

82   God presides in the heavenly council;
in the meeting of the gods he gives his
decision:
² "You must stop judging unjustly,
and quit being partial to the wicked!
³ Defend the rights of the poor and the
orphans;
be fair to the needy and the helpless.
⁴ Rescue the poor and the needy;
save them from the power of evil men!

⁵ "How ignorant you are, how stupid!
You live in darkness,
and justice has disappeared from the
world.
⁶ I told you that you are gods,
that all of you are the sons of the Most
High.
⁷ But you will die like men;
your life will end like any prince."

⁸ Come, God, and rule the world;
all the nations are yours.

A Prayer for the Defeat of Israel's Enemies

83 God, don't keep silent;
    don't be still, God, don't be quiet!
2 Look! Your enemies are in revolt,
    and those who hate you are rebelling.
3 They are making secret plans against your
    people;
    they are plotting against those you pro-
    tect.
4 "Come," they say, "let us destroy their
    nation,
    so that Israel will be forgotten forever!"

5 They agree on their plan,
    and form an alliance against you:
6 the people of Edom, and the Ishmaelites,
    the people of Moab, and the Hagrites;
7 the people of Gebal, Ammon, and Ama-
    lek,
    of Philistia and Tyre;
8 Assyria has also joined them,
    as a strong ally of the descendants of
    Lot.

9 Do to them what you did to the Midi-
    anites,
    and to Sisera and Jabin at the Kishon
    River,
10 who were defeated at Endor,
    whose bodies rotted on the ground.
11 Do to their generals what you did to Oreb
    and Zeeb;
    defeat all their rulers as you did Zebah
    and Zalmunna
12 who said, "We will take for our own
    the land that belongs to God."

13 My God, scatter them like dust,
    like straw blown away by the wind.
14 As the fire burns the forest,
    as the flames set the hills on fire,

¹⁵ so chase them away with your storm
  and terrify them with your fierce winds.
¹⁶ Cover their faces with shame, Lord,
  so they will want to serve you.
¹⁷ May they be defeated and terrified
  forever;
  may they die in complete disgrace!
¹⁸ May they know that only you are the
  Lord,
  supreme ruler over all the earth!

Longing for God's House

84 How I love your temple, Almighty
   God!
² How I want to be there!
 I long for the courts of the Lord's temple.
  With my whole being I sing with joy to
   the living God.
³ Even the sparrows have built a nest,
  and the swallows have their own home;
 they keep their young near your altars,
  Lord Almighty, my king and my God.
⁴ How happy are those who live in your
  temple,
  always singing praise to you!

⁵ How happy are those whose strength
  comes from you,
  who are eager to make the pilgrimage to
   Mount Zion.
⁶ As they pass through the dry valley
  it becomes a place of springs;
  the early rain fills it with pools.
⁷ They grow stronger as they go;
  they will see the God of gods on Zion!

⁸ Hear my prayer, Lord God Almighty;
  listen, God of Jacob!
⁹ Bless our king, God,
  the king you have chosen!

¹⁰ One day spent in your temple
     is better than a thousand anywhere else;
  I would rather stand at the gate of the
          house of my God
     than live in the homes of the wicked.
¹¹ The Lord is our protector and glorious
          king,
     blessing us with kindness and honor.
  He does not refuse any good thing
     to those who do what is right.
¹² Happy are those who trust in you,
     Almighty God!

A Prayer for the Nation's Welfare

85 Lord, you have been kind to your
          land;
     you made Israel prosperous again.
² You have forgiven your people's sins
     and pardoned all their wrongs.
³ You stopped being angry with them
     and put away your furious rage.

⁴ Bring us back, God our Savior,
     and stop being displeased with us!
⁵ Will you be angry with us forever?
     Will your anger never cease?
⁶ Please renew our strength,
     and we, your people, will praise you.
⁷ Show us your constant love, Lord,
     and give us your saving help.

⁸ I am listening to what the Lord God is
          saying;
     he promises peace to us, his own peo-
          ple,
     if we do not go back to our foolish ways.
⁹ Surely he is ready to save those who
          honor him,
     and his saving presence will remain in
          our land.

¹⁰ Love and faithfulness will come together;
    righteousness and peace will meet.
¹¹ Man's loyalty will reach up from the
    earth,
    and God's righteousness will look down
    from heaven.
¹² The Lord will make us prosperous,
    and our land will produce rich harvests.
¹³ Righteousness will go before the Lord,
    and prepare the path for him.

A Prayer for Help

86 Listen to me, Lord, and answer me,
    because I am weak and helpless.
² Save me from death, because I am loyal to
    you;
    save me, because I am your servant and
    trust in you.

³ You are my God, so be merciful to me,
    Lord;
    I pray to you all day long.
⁴ Make your servant glad, Lord,
    because my prayers go up to you.
⁵ Lord, you are good and forgiving,
    full of constant love for all who pray to
    you.

⁶ Listen, Lord, to my prayer;
    hear my cries for help.
⁷ I call to you in times of trouble,
    because you answer my prayer.

⁸ There is no other god like you, Lord,
    not one who can do what you can do.
⁹ All the nations you have created
    will come and bow down to you.
    They will praise your greatness,
¹⁰   because only you, God, are mighty;
    only you do wonderful things.

¹¹ Teach me, Lord, what you want me to do,
  and I will obey you faithfully;
    teach me to serve you with complete
      devotion.
¹² I will praise you with all my heart, Lord
    my God;
  I will proclaim your greatness forever.
¹³ How great is your constant love for me!
  You have saved me from the depths of
    the grave.
¹⁴ God, arrogant men are coming against
    me;
  a gang of cruel men is trying to kill me,
  people who pay no attention to you.
¹⁵ Lord, you are a merciful and loving God,
  slow to anger, always kind and faithful.
¹⁶ Turn to me and have mercy on me;
  strengthen me and save me,
    because I serve you, just as my mother
      did.
¹⁷ Show me proof of your goodness, Lord;
  then those who hate me will be
    ashamed,
  when they see that you have given me
    comfort and help.

In Praise of Jerusalem

87 God built his city on the sacred hills;
    ² he loves the city of Jerusalem
  more than any other place in Israel.
³ Listen, city of God,
  to the wonderful things he says about
    you:

⁴ "When I list the nations that obey me,
  I will include Egypt and Babylonia;
  and I will say of Philistia, Tyre, and Ethi-
    opia,
  that they also belong to Jerusalem."
⁵ Of Zion it will be said
  that all nations belong there,

and the Most High will make her
strong.
6 The Lord will write a list of the peoples,
  and include them all as citizens of Jerusalem.
7 All who live *m* there will sing and dance.

A Cry for Help

88 Lord God, my Savior, I cry out all
     day,
   and at night I come before you.
2 Hear my prayer;
  listen to my cry for help!

3 So many troubles have fallen on me
  that I am close to death.
4 I am like all others who are about to die;
  all my strength is gone.
5 I am abandoned among the dead;
  I am like the slain lying in their graves,
 whom you have forgotten completely,
  who are beyond your help.
6 You have thrown me into the depths of
    the tomb,
  into the darkest and deepest pit.
7 Your anger lies heavy on me,
  and I am crushed beneath its waves.

8 You have caused my friends to abandon
    me;
  you have made me repulsive to them.
 I am closed in and cannot escape;
9   my eyes are weak from suffering.
 Lord, every day I call to you,
  and lift my hands to you in prayer!

10 Do you perform miracles for the dead?
   Do they rise up and praise you?
11 Is your constant love spoken of in the
    grave,

m Some ancient translations who live; *Hebrew* their fountains.

or your faithfulness in the place of destruction?
[12] Are your miracles seen in that place of
darkness,
or your goodness in the land of doom?

[13] Lord, I call to you for help;
every morning I pray to you.
[14] Why do you reject me, Lord?
Why do you hide yourself from me?
[15] Ever since I was young I have suffered and
been near death;
I am worn out[n] from the burden of your
punishments.
[16] Your furious anger rolls over me;
your terrible attacks destroy me.
[17] All day long they surround me like a
flood;
they close in on me from all sides.
[18] You have made even my closest friends
abandon me;
darkness is the only companion I have
left.

A Hymn in Time of National Trouble

89 Lord, I will always sing of your constant love;
at all times I will proclaim your faithfulness.
[2] I know that your love will last forever,
that your faithfulness is as permanent as
the sky.
[3] You said, "I have made a covenant with
the man I chose;
I have promised my servant David,
[4] 'A descendant of yours will always be
king;
I will preserve your kingdom forever.'"

[n] Hebrew unclear.

⁵ The gods in heaven sing of the wonderful
   things you do;
      they sing of your faithfulness, Lord.
⁶ No one in heaven is like you, Lord;
      none of the gods is your equal.
⁷ You are respected in the council of the
   gods,
      and greatly feared by all around you.

⁸ Lord God Almighty, none is as mighty as
   you;
      in all things you are faithful, Lord.
⁹ You rule over the powerful sea;
      you calm its angry waves.
¹⁰ You crushed the monster Rahab and
   killed it;
      with your mighty strength you defeated
      your enemies.
¹¹ The earth is yours, and heaven also;
      you created the world and everything in
      it;
¹² you made the north and the south;
      Mount Tabor and Mount Hermon sing
      to you for joy.
¹³ How powerful you are!
      How great is your strength!
¹⁴ Your kingdom is founded on righteousness and justice;
      love and faithfulness are in all you do.

¹⁵ Happy are the people who worship you
   with songs,
      who live in the light of your kindness.
¹⁶ Because of you they rejoice all day long
      and praise you because of your good-
      ness.
¹⁷ You give us great victories;
      in your kindness you make us trium-
      phant,
¹⁸ because you chose our protector;
      you, the Holy One of Israel, gave us our
      king.

God's Promise to David

¹⁹ In a vision long ago you said to your faith-
ful servants,
"I have put the crown° on a famous
soldier;
I have given the throne to one chosen
from the people.
²⁰ I have selected my servant David
and made him your king.
²¹ My strength will always be with him,
my power will make him strong.
²² His enemies will never succeed against
him,
the wicked will not defeat him.
²³ I will crush his foes
and kill all who hate him.
²⁴ I will always love him and be loyal to him;
I will make him always victorious.
²⁵ I will extend his kingdom
from the Mediterranean Sea to the Euphrates River.
²⁶ He will say to me,
'You are my father and my God;
you are my protector and Savior.'
²⁷ I will make him my firstborn son,
the greatest of all kings.
²⁸ I will always keep my promise to him,
and my covenant with him will last
forever.
²⁹ A descendant of his will always be king;
his kingdom will be as permanent as the
sky.

³⁰ "But if his descendants disobey my law,
and do not live according to my rules;
³¹ if they disregard my instructions,
and do not keep my commandments,
³² then I will punish them for their sins;
I will whip them for their wrongs.
³³ But I will not stop loving David,

°crown; *Hebrew* help.

or fail to keep my promise to him.
³⁴ I will not break my covenant with him,
    or take back even one promise I made
    to him.

³⁵ "Once and for all I have promised by my
    holy name:
    I will never lie to David!
³⁶ He will always have descendants,
    and I will watch over his kingdom as
    long as the sun shines.
³⁷ It will be as permanent as the moon,
    as that faithful witness in the sky."

Lament over the Defeat of the King

³⁸ But you are angry with your chosen king;
    you have deserted and rejected him.
³⁹ You have canceled your covenant with
    your servant,
    and thrown his crown in the dirt.
⁴⁰ You have broken down the walls of his
    city,
    and left his forts in ruins.
⁴¹ All who pass by steal his belongings;
    all his neighbors make fun of him.
⁴² You have given the victory to his enemies;
    you have made them all happy.
⁴³ You have made his weapons useless,
    and let him be defeated in battle.
⁴⁴ You have taken away his royal scepter,^p
    and knocked his throne to the ground,
⁴⁵ You have made him old before his time,
    and covered him with disgrace.

A Prayer for Deliverance

⁴⁶ How long will you hide yourself, Lord?
    Forever?
    How long will your anger burn like fire?
⁴⁷ Remember, Lord,^q how short is man's life;

---

^proyal scepter; *Hebrew* purity.   ^qLord; *Hebrew* me.

remember that you created all men
mortal!
⁴⁸ Who can live and never die?
How can man keep himself from the
grave?

⁴⁹ Lord, where are the former proofs of your
love?
Where are the promises you made to
David?
⁵⁰ Don't forget how I, your servant, am insulted;
how I endure all the insults of the heathen.
⁵¹ How your enemies insult your chosen
king, Lord!
They insult him wherever he goes.

⁵² Let us praise the Lord forever!
Amen! Amen!

BOOK FOUR
(Psalms 90–106)

Of God and Man

90 Lord, you have always been our
home.
² Before the hills were created,
before you brought the world into being,
you are eternally God, without beginning or end.

³ You tell men to return to what they were;
you change them back to soil.
⁴ A thousand years to you are like one day;
they are like yesterday, already gone,

insults; *Hebrew* crowds.

like a short hour in the night.
⁵ You carry men away like a flood;
   they last no longer than a dream.
They are like weeds that sprout in the
     morning,
⁶   that grow and burst into bloom,
   then dry up and die in the evening.

⁷ We are destroyed by your anger;
   we are terrified by your fury.
⁸ You place our sins before you,
   our secret sins where you can see them.

⁹ Our lifetime is cut short by your anger;
   our life comes to an end like a whisper.
¹⁰ Seventy years is all we have—
   eighty years, if we are strong;
yet all they bring us is worry and trouble;
   life is soon over, and we are gone.

¹¹ Who really knows the full power of your
     anger?
   Who knows what fear your fury can
     bring?
¹² Teach us how short our life is,
   so that we may become wise.

¹³ How long, Lord, before you relent?
   Have pity on your servants!
¹⁴ Fill us each morning with your constant
     love,
   that we may sing and be glad all our life.
¹⁵ Give us now as much happiness as you
     gave us sadness,
   during all those years when we had
     troubles.
¹⁶ Let us, your servants, see your mighty
     acts;
   let our descendants see your glorious
     might.
¹⁷ Lord our God, may your blessings be with
     us,

and give us success in all we do!
Yes, give us success in all we do!

God Our Protector

91 Whoever goes to the Most High for
safety,
whoever remains under the protection
of the Almighty,
² can say to the Lord,
"You are my defender and protector!
You are my God; in you I trust."

³ He will surely keep you safe from all hidden dangers,
and from all deadly diseases.
⁴ He will cover you with his wings;
you will be safe under his care;
his faithfulness will protect and defend
you.
⁵ You will not be afraid of dangers at night,
or of sudden attacks during the day,
⁶ of the plagues that strike in the dark,
or of the evils that kill in daylight.

⁷ A thousand may fall beside you,
ten thousand all around you,
but you will not be harmed.
⁸ You will look and see
how the wicked are punished.

⁹ Because you made the Lord your defender,
the Most High your protector,
¹⁰ no disaster will strike you,
no violence will come near your home.
¹¹ God will put his angels in charge of you,
to protect you wherever you go.
¹² They will hold you up with their hands,
to keep you from hurting your feet on
the rocks.

¹³ You will trample down lions and snakes,
　　fierce lions and poisonous snakes.

¹⁴ God says, "I will save those who love me,
　　and protect those who know me.
¹⁵ When they call to me, I will answer them;
　　when they are in trouble, I will be with
　　　them.
　I will rescue them and honor them.
¹⁶ I will reward them with long life,
　　and will surely save them."

A Song of Praise

92 How good it is to give thanks to the
　　　Lord,
　　to sing in your honor, Most High God,
² to proclaim your constant love every
　　morning,
　　and your faithfulness every night,
³ with the music of stringed instruments,
　　and with melody on the harp.
⁴ Your mighty acts, Lord, make me glad;
　　because of what you have done I sing
　　　for joy.

⁵ How great are your acts, Lord!
　　How deep are your thoughts!
⁶ Here is something a fool cannot know,
　　a stupid man cannot understand:
⁷ the wicked may grow like weeds,
　　and all evildoers may prosper;
　yet they will be totally destroyed,
⁸ 　because you, Lord, are supreme for-
　　　ever.

⁹ We know that your enemies will die,
　　and all wicked men be defeated.
¹⁰ You have made me as strong as a wild
　　bull;
　　you have blessed me with happiness.

¹¹ I have seen the defeat of my enemies,
and heard the cries of the wicked.

¹² The righteous will flourish like palm trees;
they will grow like the cedars of Lebanon.
¹³ They are like trees planted in the house of
the Lord,
that flourish in the temple of our God,
¹⁴   that still bear fruit in old age,
and are always green and strong.
¹⁵ This shows that the Lord is just;
in him, my defender, there is no wrong.

God the King

93 The Lord is king!
He is clothed with majesty,
and covered with strength.
Surely the earth is set firmly in place
and cannot be moved.
² Your throne, Lord, has been firm from the
beginning,
and you existed before time began.

³ The ocean depths raise their voice, Lord;
they raise their voice and roar.
⁴ The Lord rules supreme in heaven,
greater than the roar of the ocean,
more powerful than the waves of the
sea.

⁵ Your laws are eternal, Lord,
and your temple is holy indeed,
forever and ever.

God the Judge of All

94 Lord, you are a God who punishes;
reveal[s] your anger!
² You are the judge of all men;

[s] *Some ancient translations* reveal; *Hebrew* you revealed.

rise and give the proud what they deserve!
3 How much longer will the wicked be glad?
How much longer, Lord?
4 How much longer will evildoers be proud
and boast about their crimes?

5 They crush your people, Lord;
they oppress those who belong to you.
6 They kill widows and orphans,
and murder the strangers who live in
our land.
7 They say, "The Lord doesn't see us;
the God of Israel does not notice!"

8 My people, how can you be such stupid
fools?
When will you ever learn?
9 God made our ears—can't he hear?
He made our eyes—can't he see?
10 He is in charge of the nations—won't he
punish them?
He is the teacher of all men—doesn't he
know?
11 The Lord knows what they think;
he knows how senseless their reasoning
is.

12 Lord, happy is the man whom you instruct,
the man to whom you teach your law,
13 to give him rest from days of trouble,
until a grave is dug for the wicked.
14 The Lord will not abandon his people;
he will not desert those who belong to
him.
15 Justice will again be found in courts of
judgment,
and all righteous people will support it.

16 Who stood up for me against the wicked?
Who took my side against the evildoers?

¹⁷ If the Lord had not helped me,
> I would have gone quickly to the land
> of silence.

¹⁸ I said, "I am falling";
> but, Lord, your constant love held me
> up.

¹⁹ When I am anxious and worried,
> you comfort me and make me glad.

²⁰ You have nothing to do with corrupt
> judges,
> who make injustice legal,

²¹ who plot against good men,
> and sentence the innocent to death.

²² But the Lord defends me;
> my God protects me.

²³ He will punish them for their wickedness,
> and destroy them for their sins;
> the Lord our God will destroy them.

A Song of Praise

95 Come, let us praise the Lord!
> Let us sing for joy to our protector
> and Savior!

² Let us come before him with thanksgiv-
> ing,
> and sing joyful songs of praise!

³ For the Lord is a mighty God,
> a mighty king over all the gods.

⁴ He rules over the whole earth,
> from the deepest caves to the highest
> hills.

⁵ He rules over the sea, which he made;
> the land also, which he himself formed.

⁶ Come, let us bow down and worship him;
> let us kneel before the Lord, our Maker!

⁷ He is our God;
> we are the people he looks after,
> the flock for which he provides.

Let us praise the Lord!

Listen today to what he says:
8 "Don't be stubborn, as your ancestors
were at Meribah,
as they were that day in the desert at
Massah.
9 There they put me to the test and tried
me,
although they had seen what I did for
them.
10 For forty years I was disgusted with those
people;
I said, 'How disloyal they are!
They refuse to obey my commands!'

¹¹ I was angry and made a solemn promise,
    'You will never enter the land where I
      would give you rest.' "

God the Supreme King

96   Sing a new song to the Lord!
      Sing to the Lord, all the world!
² Sing to the Lord, and praise him!
    Every day tell the good news that he
      has saved us!
³ Proclaim his glory to the nations,
    his mighty acts to all peoples.

⁴ The Lord is great, and must be highly
      praised;
    he must be feared more than all the
      gods.
⁵ The gods of all other nations are only
      idols,
    but the Lord made the heavens.
⁶ Glory and majesty are around him,
    greatness and beauty are in his temple.

⁷ All people on earth, praise the Lord!
    Praise his glory and might!
⁸ Praise the Lord's glorious name;
    bring an offering and come into his tem-
      ple.
⁹ Bow down before the Holy One when he
      appears;
    tremble before him, all the earth!

¹⁰ Say to all the nations, "The Lord is king!
    The earth is set firmly in place and can-
      not be moved;
    he will judge all peoples with justice."
¹¹ Be glad, earth and sky!
    Roar, sea, and all the creatures in you;
¹²   be glad, fields, and everything in you!
    Then the trees in the woods will shout for

joy before the Lord,
13 because he comes to rule the earth.
He will rule all peoples of the world
with justice and fairness.

God the Supreme Ruler

97 The Lord is king! Be glad, earth!
Rejoice, all you islands of the
seas!
2 Clouds and darkness are around him;
his kingdom is based on righteousness
and justice.
3 Fire goes in front of him,
and burns up his enemies around him.
4 His lightning lights up the world;
the earth sees it and trembles.
5 The hills melt like wax before the Lord,
before the Lord of all the earth.
6 The heavens proclaim his righteousness,
and all peoples see his glory.

7 All who worship images are ashamed,
all who boast of their idols;
all the gods bow down before him.
8 The people of Zion are glad,
and the cities of Judah rejoice,
because of your judgments, Lord!
9 Lord Almighty, you are ruler of all the
earth;
you are much greater than all the gods.

10 The Lord loves those who hate evil;*
he protects the lives of his people,
he rescues them from the power of the
wicked.
11 Light shines on the righteous,
and gladness on the good.
12 All you that are righteous, be glad,
because of what the Lord has done!

*The Lord loves those who hate evil; *Hebrew* Hate evil, you who love
the Lord.

Remember what the Holy One has done,
    and give thanks to him!

God the Ruler of the World

98 Sing a new song to the Lord;
        he has done wonderful things!
By his own power and holy strength,
    he has won the victory.
² The Lord announced his victory;
    he made his saving power known to the
        nations.
³ He kept his promise to the people of
    Israel,
    with constant love and loyalty for them.
All people everywhere have seen the vic-
    tory of our God!

⁴ Sing for joy to the Lord, all the earth;
    praise him with songs and shouts of joy!
⁵ Sing praises to the Lord with harps;
    play music on the harps!
⁶ With trumpets and horns,
    shout for joy before the Lord, the king!

⁷ Roar, sea, and all creatures in you;
    sing, earth, and all who live there!
⁸ Clap your hands, oceans;
    hills, sing together with joy before the
    Lord,
ᵛ   because he comes to rule the earth!
He will rule all peoples of the world
    with justice and fairness.

God the Supreme King

99 The Lord is king;
        the people tremble;
he sits on his throne on the cherubim;
    the earth shakes.
² The Lord is mighty in Zion;
    he rules over all the nations.

3 Everyone will praise his great and majes-
    tic name.
    Holy is he!

4 Mighty king,[u] you love what is right;
    you have brought justice to Israel;
    you have brought righteousness and
       fairness.
5 Praise the Lord our God;
    worship before his throne!
    Holy is he!

6 Moses and Aaron were his priests,
    and Samuel was one who worshiped
       him;
    they called to the Lord and he answered
       them.
7 He spoke to them from the column of
       cloud;
    they obeyed the laws and command-
       ments that he gave them.

8 Lord, our God, you answered your peo-
       ple;
    you showed them that you are a God
       who forgives,
    but you punished them for their sins.
9 Praise the Lord our God
    and worship at his sacred mountain!
    The Lord our God is holy!

A Hymn of Praise

100   Sing for joy to the Lord, all the
       world!
2 Worship the Lord gladly,
    and come before him with joyful songs!

3 Never forget that the Lord is God!
    He made us, and we belong to him;
    we are his people, we are his flock.

[u]Mighty king; *Hebrew* The might of the king.

⁴ Enter his temple with thanksgiving,
      go into his sanctuary with praise!
    Give thanks to him and praise him!

⁵ The Lord is good;
      his love lasts forever,
    and his faithfulness for all time.

A King's Promise

101   My song is about loyalty and jus-
              tice,
      and I sing it to you, Lord.
² My conduct will be faultless.
    When will you come to me?

  I will live a pure life in my house;
³   I will never tolerate evil.

  I hate the actions of those who turn away
        from God;
    I will have nothing to do with them.
⁴ I will not be dishonest;
    I will not even think of evil.

⁵ I will destroy a man
      who whispers evil things about his
        friend;
  I will not tolerate a man
      who is proud and arrogant.

⁶ I will approve of those who are faithful to
        God,
      and let them live in my palace;
    those who are completely honest
      will be allowed to serve me.

⁷ No liar will live in my palace;
      no hypocrite will remain in my pres-
        ence.
⁸ Day after day I will destroy
      all the wicked in our land;

I will expel all evil men
   from the city of the Lord.

The Prayer of a Troubled Man[v]

102 Listen to my prayer, Lord,
   and hear my cry for help!
2 Don't hide yourself from me
   when I am in trouble!
Listen to me,
   and answer me quickly when I call!

3 My life disappears like smoke;
   my body burns like fire.
4 I am beaten down like dry grass;
   I have lost my desire for food.
5 I groan aloud;
   I am nothing but skin and bones.
6 I am like a wild bird in the desert,
   like an owl in abandoned ruins.
7 I lie awake;
   I am like a lonely bird on a housetop.
8 All day long my enemies insult me;
   those who make fun of me use my name
     in cursing.

9 Ashes are my food,
   and my tears are mixed with my drink,
10   because of your anger and fury.
You picked me up and threw me away.
11 My life is like the evening shadows;
   I am like dry grass.

12 But you, Lord, are king forever;
   all generations will remember you.
13 You will rise and take pity on Zion;
   the time has come to have mercy on
     her;

[v]*Hebrew title:* The prayer of a man in trouble who in distress pours
out his complaint to the Lord.

this is the right time!

14 Your servants love her, even though she is
destroyed;
they have pity on her, even though she
is in ruins.

15 The nations will fear the Lord;
all the kings of the earth will fear his
power.
16 When the Lord rebuilds Zion,
he will reveal his greatness.
17 He will hear his abandoned people
and listen to their prayer.

18 Write down for the coming generation
what the Lord did,
so that people not yet born will praise
him.
19 The Lord looked down from his holy
place on high,
he looked down from heaven to the
earth,
20 to hear the groans of prisoners,
and to set free those who were condemned to die.
21 And so men will proclaim the name of the
Lord in Zion;
they will give thanks to him in Jerusalem,
22 when nations and kingdoms come
together
and worship the Lord.

23 The Lord made me weak while I was still
young;
he has shortened my life.
24 My God, do not take me away now,
before I grow old!

Lord, you live forever;
25 long ago you created the earth,
and with your own hands you made the
heavens.

²⁶ They will all disappear, but you will re-
    main;
  they will all wear out like clothes.
  You will change them like clothes, and
    they will vanish;
²⁷ but you are always the same, and your
    life never ends.
²⁸ Our children will live in safety,
    and their descendants will always live
    under your protection.

The Love of God

103 Praise the Lord, my soul!
        All my being, praise his holy
        name!
² Praise the Lord, my soul,
    and do not forget how kind he is.
³ He forgives all my sins
    and heals all my diseases;
⁴ he saves me from the grave
    and blesses me with love and mercy;
⁵ he fills my life*ʷ* with good things,
    so that I stay young and strong like an
    eagle.

⁶ The Lord judges in favor of the oppressed
    and gives them their rights.
⁷ He told his plans to Moses
    and let the people of Israel see his
    mighty acts.
⁸ The Lord is merciful and loving,
    slow to become angry, and full of con-
    stant love.
⁹ He does not keep on reprimanding;
    he is not angry forever.
¹⁰ He does not punish us as we deserve,
    or repay us for our sins and wrongs.
¹¹ As high as the sky is above the earth,
    so great is his love for those who fear
    him.

ʷmy life; *Hebrew unclear.*

¹² As far as the east is from the west,
    so far does he remove our sins from us.
¹³ As kind as a father is to his children,
    so the Lord is kind to those who fear
      him.
¹⁴ He knows what we are made of;
    he remembers that we are dust.

The wind blows on it, and it is gone

¹⁵ As for man, his life is like grass;
  he grows and flourishes like a wild
    flower.
¹⁶ Then the wind blows on it, and it is gone,
  and no one sees it again.
¹⁷ But the Lord's love for those who honor
    him lasts forever,
  and his goodness endures for all genera-
    tions,
¹⁸ to those who are true to his covenant,
  and who faithfully obey his command-
    ments.

¹⁹ The Lord set up his throne in heaven;
  he is king over all.
²⁰ Praise the Lord, you strong and mighty
    angels,
  who obey his commands,
  who listen to what he says!
²¹ Praise the Lord, all you heavenly powers,
  you servants who do what he wants!
²² Praise the Lord, all his creatures,
  in every place he rules!
  Praise the Lord, my soul!

In Praise of the Creator

104 Praise the Lord, my soul!
      Lord, my God, how great you
        are!
  You are clothed with majesty and glory;
²   you cover yourself with light.
  You stretched out the heavens like a tent,
³   and built your home on the waters
      above.
  You use the clouds as your chariot,
    and walk on the wings of the wind.
⁴ You use the winds as your messengers,
    and flashes of lightning as your serv-
      ants.

⁵ You have set the earth firmly on its foun-
    dations,

and it will never be moved.
⁶ You placed the ocean over it like a robe,
and the water covered the mountains;
⁷ but when you reprimanded the waters,
they fled;
when they heard your shout of command, they rushed away.
⁸ They went over the mountains down into the valleys,
to the place you had made for them;
⁹ you set a boundary they can never pass,
to keep them from covering the earth again.

¹⁰ You make springs flow in the valleys,
and water run between the hills.
¹¹ They provide water for the wild animals;
the wild donkeys quench their thirst;
¹² in the trees near by
the birds make their nests and sing.

¹³ From heaven you send rain on the mountains,
and the earth is filled with your blessings.
¹⁴ You make grass grow for the cattle,
and plants for man to use,
so he can grow his crops,
¹⁵ and produce wine to make him happy,
olive oil to make him cheerful,
and bread to give him strength.

¹⁶ The cedars of Lebanon get plenty of rain,
the Lord's own trees, which he planted.
¹⁷ There the birds build their nests;
the storks nest in the fir trees.
¹⁸ The wild goats live in the high mountains,
and the badgers hide in the cliffs.

¹⁹ You created the moon to mark the months;
the sun knows the time to set.

You make springs flow in the valley

²⁰ You made the night, and in the darkness
     all the wild animals come out.
²¹ The young lions roar while they hunt,
     looking for the food that God gives
       them.
²² When the sun rises they go back
     and lie down in their dens.
²³ Then men go out to do their work,
     and keep working until evening.

²⁴ Lord, you have made so many things!
     How wisely you made them all!
     The earth is filled with your creatures.
²⁵ There is the ocean, large and wide,
     where countless creatures live,
     large and small alike;
²⁶ the ships sail on it, and Leviathan plays in
       it,
     that sea monster which you made.

²⁷ All of them depend on you,
     to give them food when they need it.
²⁸ You give it to them, and they eat it;
     you provide food, and they are satisfied.
²⁹ When you turn away, they are afraid;
     when you hold back your breath, they
       die,
     and go back to the soil they came from.
³⁰ But when you give them breath, they live;
     you give new life to the earth.

³¹ May the glory of the Lord last forever!
     May the Lord be happy with what he
       made!
³² He looks at the earth, and it trembles;
     he touches the mountains, and they
       pour out smoke.

³³ I will sing to the Lord all my life;
     I will sing praises to my God as long as
       I live.
³⁴ May he be pleased with my song,

because he makes me glad.
35 May sinners be destroyed from the earth;
   may the wicked be no more!

Praise the Lord, my soul!
Praise the Lord!

God and His People

105 Give thanks to the Lord, proclaim
    his greatness,
   and make known to the nations what he
   has done!
2 Sing to him, sing praise to him;
   tell all the wonderful things he has
   done!
3 Be glad that we belong to him;
   let all who serve the Lord rejoice!
4 Go to the Lord for help;
   stay in his presence always.
5-6 You descendants of Abraham, his servant,
   you descendants of Jacob, his chosen
   one:
   remember his great and wonderful miracles,
   and the judgments he gave.

7 He, the Lord, is our God;
   his commands are for all the world.
8 He will keep his covenant forever,
   his promises for a thousand generations,
9 the agreement he made with Abraham,
   and his promise to Isaac.
10 The Lord made an eternal covenant with
   Israel,
   a lasting agreement with Jacob, when
   he said,
11 "I will give you the land of Canaan;
   it will be your own possession."

12 God's people were few in number,

and they were strangers in the land.
¹³ They wandered from country to country,
from one kingdom to another,
¹⁴ but he did not let anyone oppress them,
and he reprimanded kings on their account.
¹⁵ He said, "Don't touch my chosen servants;
do not harm my prophets!"

¹⁶ When the Lord sent famine to their country,
and took away all their food,
¹⁷ he sent Joseph ahead of them,
who had been sold as a slave.
¹⁸ His feet were hurt by tight chains,
and an iron collar was put around his neck,
¹⁹ until what he had predicted came true.
The word of the Lord proved him right.
²⁰ Then the king of Egypt had him released;
the ruler of nations set him free.
²¹ He put him in charge of his government,
and made him ruler over all the land,
²² with complete authority over the king's officials,
and power to instruct his advisers.

²³ Then Jacob went to Egypt,
and settled in that country.
²⁴ The Lord let his people have many children,
and made them stronger than their enemies.
²⁵ He made the Egyptians hate his people,
and act deceitfully with his servants.

²⁶ Then he sent his servant Moses,
and Aaron, whom he chose.
²⁷ They did God's mighty acts,
and performed miracles in Egypt.
²⁸ He sent darkness on the land,

but the Egyptians did not obey[x] his
command.
29 He turned their rivers into blood,
and killed all their fish.
30 Their country was filled with frogs,
even the king's palace.
31 God commanded, and flies and gnats
filled the whole country.
32 He sent hail and lightning on their land,
instead of rain;
33 he destroyed their grapevines and fig
trees,
and broke down the trees.
34 He commanded, and the grasshoppers
came,
countless millions of them;
35 they ate all the plants in the land;
they ate all the crops.
36 He killed the firstborn sons
of all the families of Egypt.

37 Then he led the Israelites out;
they carried silver and gold,
and all of them were strong and
healthy.
38 The Egyptians were glad when they left,
because they were afraid of them.
39 He put a cloud over his people
and a fire to give them light by night.
40 They[y] asked, and he sent quails,
he gave them food from heaven to satisfy them.
41 He opened a rock, and water gushed out,
flowing through the desert like a river.
42 He remembered his sacred promise
to Abraham his servant.

43 So he led his people out with singing,
his chosen people with shouts of joy.
44 He gave them the lands of foreigners,

Some ancient translations did not obey; *Hebrew* obeyed. *Some ancient translations* They; *Hebrew* He.

and let them take over their fields,
⁴⁵ so that his people would obey his laws,
and keep his commandments.

Praise the Lord!

The Lord's Goodness to His People

106   Praise the Lord!

Give thanks to the Lord, because he is
good;
his love is eternal.
² Who can tell all the great things he has
done?
Who can praise him enough?
³ Happy are those who obey his command,
who always do what is right!

⁴ Remember me, Lord, when you help your
people;
include me, when you save them.
⁵ Let me see the prosperity of your people,
and share in the happiness of your nation,
in the glad pride of those who belong to
you.

⁶ We have sinned, as our ancestors did;
we have been wicked and evil.
⁷ Our ancestors in Egypt did not understand God's wonderful acts;
they forgot the many times he showed
his love for them,
and they rebelled against the Almighty*z*
at the Sea of Reeds.
⁸ But he saved them, as he had promised,
in order to show his great power.
⁹ He commanded the Sea of Reeds, and it
dried up,

*z*the Almighty; *Hebrew* against the sea.

and he led his people across it as though
   on dry land.
10 He saved them from those who hated
   them;
   he rescued them from their enemies.
11 The water drowned their enemies;
   not one of them was left.
12 Then his people believed his promises,
   and sang praise to him.

13 But they quickly forgot what he had done,
   and acted without waiting for his advice.
14 They were filled with desire in the desert,
   and put God to the test;
15 so he gave them what they asked for,
   but sent a terrible disease among them.

16 There in the desert they were jealous of
   Moses,
   and of Aaron, the Lord's holy servant;
17 then the earth opened up and swallowed
   Dathan,
   and buried Abiram and his family;
18 fire came down on their followers,
   and burned up those wicked people.

19 They made a gold calf at Horeb,
   and worshiped this image;
20 they exchanged the glory of God
   for the image of an animal that eats
   grass.
21 They forgot the God who had saved them,
   by his mighty acts in Egypt.
22 What wonderful things he did there!
   What amazing things he did at the Sea
   of Reeds!
23 And so God said he would destroy his
   people;
   but Moses, his chosen servant, stood up
   against God,
   and kept his anger from destroying
   them.

²⁴ Then they refused the pleasant land,
   because they did not believe God's
      promise.
²⁵ They stayed in their tents and grumbled,
   and would not listen to the Lord.
²⁶ So he gave them a solemn warning
   that he would make them die in the
      desert,
²⁷ and scatter their descendants among the
      heathen,
   letting them die in foreign countries.

²⁸ Then God's people joined in the worship
      of Baal, at Peor,
   and ate the sacrifices offered to dead
      gods.
²⁹ They stirred up the Lord's anger by their
      actions,
   and a terrible disease broke out among
      them;
³⁰ but Phinehas stood up and punished the
      guilty,
   and the plague was stopped,
³¹ and this has been remembered in his favor
      ever since,
   and will be for all time to come.

³² The Lord's people made him angry at the
      springs of Meribah,
   and Moses was in trouble on their ac-
      count.
³³ They made Moses so bitter,
   that he said things he shouldn't have
      said.

³⁴ They did not kill the heathen,
   as the Lord had commanded,
³⁵ but intermarried with them,
   and imitated their pagan ways.
³⁶ God's people worshiped idols,
   and this caused their destruction.
³⁷ They offered their own sons and daugh-
      ters

as sacrifices to pagan gods;
³⁸ they killed these innocent people,
their own sons and daughters,
as a sacrifice to the idols of Canaan;
the land was made impure by these kill-
ings.
³⁹ They defiled themselves by their actions,
and were unfaithful to God.

⁴⁰ So the Lord was angry with his people;
he was disgusted with them.
⁴¹ He abandoned them to the power of the
heathen,
and their enemies ruled over them.
⁴² They were oppressed by their enemies,
and were in complete subjection to
them.
⁴³ Many times the Lord rescued his people,
but they chose to rebel against him,
and sank deeper into sin,
⁴⁴ Yet the Lord heard them when they cried
out,
and took notice of their distress.
⁴⁵ For their sake he remembered his cove-
nant,
and because of his great love he
changed his mind.
⁴⁶ He made those who held them prisoners
feel sorry for them.

⁴⁷ Save us, Lord our God,
and bring us back from among the nations,
so that we may praise your holy name,
and be happy in thanking you.

⁴⁸ Let us praise the Lord, the God of Israel;
praise him now and forever!
All the people are to say, "Amen!"

Praise the Lord!

BOOK FIVE
(Psalms 107–150)

In Praise of God's Goodness

107 Give thanks to the Lord, because
he is good;
his love is eternal!
2 Join me in praising the Lord,
all you whom he has saved.
He has rescued you from your enemies,
and brought you back from foreign
countries,
from east and west, from north and
south.*

4 Some wandered in the trackless desert,
and could not find their way to a city to
live in;
5 they were hungry and thirsty,
and had given up all hope.
6 In their trouble they called to the Lord,
and he saved them from their distress.
7 He led them out,
straight to a city to live in.
8 They must thank the Lord for his constant
love,
for the wonderful things he did for
them!
9 He satisfies those who are thirsty,
and the hungry he fills with good things.

10 Some were living in gloom and darkness,
prisoners suffering in chains,
11 because they had rebelled against the
commands of Almighty God,
and had rejected his instructions.
12 They were worn out from hard work;

*south; *Hebrew* the sea (*meaning* "west").

they would fall down, and no one would
help.

13 In their trouble they called to the Lord,
and he saved them from their distress.

14 He brought them out of their gloom and
darkness,
and smashed their chains.

15 They must thank the Lord for his constant
love,
for the wonderful things he did for
them.

16 He breaks down bronze doors,
and smashes iron bars.

17 Some were sick[b] because of their sins,
suffering because of their evil;

18 they couldn't stand the sight of food,
and were close to dying.

19 In their trouble they called to the Lord,
and he saved them from their distress.

20 He healed them with his command,
and saved them from the grave.

21 They must thank the Lord for his constant
love,
for the wonderful things he did for
them.

22 They must thank him with sacrifices,
and with songs of joy tell all he has
done!

23 Some sailed over the ocean in ships,
earning their living on the seas;

24 they saw what the Lord has done,
his wonderful acts on the seas.

25 He commanded, and a mighty wind began
to blow
and stirred up the waves.

26 The ships were lifted high in the air and
plunged down into the depths;
in such danger, the men lost their courage;

[b]sick; *Hebrew* fools.

²⁷ they stumbled and staggered like drunken
        men;
        all their skill was useless.
²⁸ In their trouble they called to the Lord,
        and he saved them from their distress.
²⁹ He made the storm be still,
        and the waves became quiet.
³⁰ They were glad because of the calm,
        and he brought them safe to the port
        they wanted.

And he brought them safe to the port

³¹ They must thank the Lord for his constant
        love,
        for the wonderful things he did for
        them.
³² They must proclaim his greatness in the
        assembly of the people,
        and praise him before the council of the
        elders.

³³ The Lord has made rivers dry up com-
        pletely,
        and stopped springs from flowing.
³⁴ He has made rich soil become a salty
        wasteland,
        because of the wickedness of those who
        lived there.

35 He has changed deserts into pools of water,
   and dry land into flowing springs.
36 He has let hungry people settle there,
   and they built a city to live in;
37 they sowed the fields and planted grapevines,
   which produced an abundant harvest.
38 He blessed his people and they had many
children,
   and he kept their herds of cattle from
   decreasing.

39 When God's people were defeated and
humiliated,
   by cruel oppression and suffering,
40 he showed his contempt for their oppressors,
   and made them wander in the trackless
   deserts.
41 But he rescued the needy from their mis-
ery,
   and made their families increase like
   flocks.
42 The righteous see this, and are glad,
   but all the wicked are put to silence.

43 May those who are wise think about these
things;
   may they acknowledge the Lord's constant love.

A Prayer for Help against Enemies
(Psalms 57.7-11; 60.5-12)

108 I am ready, God;
     I am completely ready!
   I will sing and praise you!
  Wake up, my soul!
2   Wake up, my harp and lyre!
   I will wake up the sun!

³ I will thank you among the nations, Lord!
    I will praise you among the peoples!
⁴ Your constant love reaches above the
        heavens,
    your faithfulness to the skies.

⁵ God, show your greatness in the sky,
    and your glory over all the earth!
⁶ Save us by your might; answer my prayer,
    so that the people you love may be res-
        cued.

⁷ In his sanctuary God has said,
    "In triumph I will divide Shechem,
    and distribute Succoth Valley to my
        people.
⁸ Gilead is mine, and Manasseh too;
    Ephraim is my helmet,
    and Judah my royal scepter.
⁹ But I will use Moab as my washbowl
    and Edom as my sandal box.
    I will shout in triumph over Philistia."

¹⁰ Who will take me, God, into the fortified
        city?
    Who will bring me to Edom?
¹¹ Have you really rejected us?
    Aren't you going to march out with our
        armies?
¹² Help us fight the enemy,
    because human help is worthless!
¹³ With God on our side we will win;
    he will defeat our enemies.

The Complaint of a Man in Trouble

109 I praise you, God; don't be silent!
    ² Wicked men and liars have at-
        tacked me,
    telling lies about me.
³ They say terrible things about me,
    attacking me for no reason.

4 They oppose me, even though I love
 them,
  and have prayed for them.
5 They pay me back evil for good,
  and hatred for love.

6 Choose a corrupt man to judge my enemy,
  and let one of his own enemies accuse
   him.
7 May he be tried and found guilty;
  may even his prayer be considered a
   crime!
8 May his life soon be ended;
  may another man take his job!
9 May his children become orphans,
  and his wife a widow!
10 May his children be homeless beggars;
  may they be driven from^c the ruins they
   live in!
11 May his creditors take away all his prop-
  erty,
  and strangers get everything he worked
   for.
12 May no one ever be kind to him;
  may no one take care of his orphans.
13 May all his descendants die,
  and his name be forgotten in the next
   generation.
14 May the Lord remember the evil of his
  ancestors,
  and never forgive his mother's sins.
15 May the Lord always remember their sins,
  but may they themselves be completely
   forgotten!
16 That man never thought of being kind;
  the poor, the needy, and the helpless
   he persecuted and killed.
17 He loved to curse—may he be cursed!
  He hated to bless—may no one bless
   him!
18 He cursed as easily as he dressed himself;

^cOne ancient translation be driven from; Hebrew seek.

may his curses soak into him like water,
and soak into his bones like oil!
¹⁹ May they cover him like clothes,
and be always around him like a belt.

²⁰ May this be how the Lord punishes my
enemies,
who say such terrible things against me!
²¹ But Lord, my God, help me as you have
promised,
and rescue me because of the goodness
of your love.
²² I am poor and needy;
I am hurt to the depths of my heart.
²³ I am about to vanish like an evening
shadow;
I am blown away like an insect.
²⁴ My knees are weak from lack of food;
my body is thin and feeble.
²⁵ When people see me, they make fun of
me;
they shake their heads in scorn.

²⁶ Help me, Lord my God;
save me because of your constant love!
²⁷ Make my enemies know
that you are the one who saves me.
²⁸ They may curse me, but you will bless me.
May my persecutors be defeated,^d
and may I, your servant, be glad.
²⁹ May my enemies be covered with dis-
grace;
may they wear their shame like a robe.

³⁰ I will give loud thanks to the Lord;
I will praise him in the meeting of the
people,
³¹ because he defends the poor man,
to save him from those who condemn
him to death.

^d*One ancient translation* May my persecutors be defeated; *Hebrew*
They persecuted me and were defeated.

The Lord and His Chosen King

110 The Lord said to my lord, the king,
"Sit here at my right side,
until I put your enemies under your
feet."

2 From Zion the Lord will extend your
royal power.
"Rule over your enemies," he says.

3 The day you fight your enemies
your people will volunteer.
Like the dew early in the morning,
your young men will come to you on
the sacred hills.*e*

4 The Lord made a solemn promise, and
will not take it back:
"You will be a priest forever,
in the priestly order of Melchizedek."

5 The Lord is at your right side;
he will defeat kings on the day he
becomes angry.

6 He will pass judgment on the nations,
and fill the battlefield with corpses;
he will defeat kings over the whole
earth.

7 The king will drink from the stream by the
road,
and strengthened, he will stand victorious.

In Praise of the Lord

111 Praise the Lord!

With all my heart I will thank the Lord,
in the meeting of his people.

2 How wonderful are the things the Lord
does!
All who are pleased with them want to
understand them.

eHebrew text uncertain and unclear.

³ All he does is full of honor and majesty;
  his righteousness is eternal.

⁴ The Lord does not let us forget his won-
    derful actions;
  he is kind and merciful.
⁵ He provides food for those who fear him;
  he never forgets his covenant.
⁶ He has shown his power to his people,
  by giving them the lands of foreigners.

⁷ In all he does he is faithful and just;
  all his commandments are dependable.
⁸ They last for all time;
  they were given in truth and righteous-
    ness.
⁹ He brought salvation to his people,
  and made an eternal covenant with
    them.
  Holy and mighty is he!
¹⁰ The way to become wise is to fear the
    Lord;
  he gives sound judgment to all who
    obey his commands.
He is to be praised forever!

The Happiness of a Good Person

112 Praise the Lord!

Happy is the man who fears the
    Lord,
  who takes pleasure in obeying
    his commands.
² His children will be mighty in the land;
  the good man's descendants will be
    blessed.
³ His family will be wealthy and rich,
  ' and he will be prosperous forever.

⁴ Light shines in the darkness for good men,
    for those who are kind, merciful, and
    just.

5 Happy is the man who is generous in his
      loans,
    who runs his business honestly.
6 A good man will never fail;
    he will never be forgotten.

7 He is not afraid of receiving bad news;
    his faith is strong, and he trusts in the
      Lord.
8 He is not worried or afraid;
    he is certain he will see his enemies de-
      feated.
9 He gives generously to the needy,
    and his kindness is eternal;
    he will be powerful and respected.
10 The wicked see this and are upset;
    they glare in anger and disappear;
    their hopes are gone forever.

In Praise of the Lord's Goodness

113   Praise the Lord!

  You servants of the Lord,
    praise his name!
2 His name will be praised,
    now and forever!
3 From the east to the west,
    the Lord's name be praised!
4 The Lord rules over all nations,
    his glory is above the heavens.

5 There is no one like the Lord our God;
    he lives in the heights above,
6 but he bends down
    to see the heavens and the earth.
7 He raises the poor from the dust;
    he lifts the needy from their misery,
8 and makes them companions of princes,
    the princes of his people.
9 He honors the childless wife in her home;

he makes her happy by giving her **children.**

Praise the Lord!

A Passover Song

114 When the people of Israel left
Egypt,
when Jacob's descendants left that foreign land,
² Judah became the Lord's holy people,
Israel became his own possession.

³ The Sea of Reeds looked and ran **away,**
the Jordan River stopped flowing.
⁴ The mountains skipped like goats,
the hills skipped around like sheep.

⁵ What happened, Sea, to make you run
away?
And you, Jordan, why did you stop
flowing?
⁶ Mountains, why did you skip like goats?
Hills, why did you skip around like
sheep?

⁷ Tremble, earth, at the Lord's coming,
at the presence of the God of Jacob,
⁸ who changes rocks into pools of water,
and stone cliffs into flowing springs.

The One True God

115 To you alone, Lord, to you alone,
and not to us, must glory be
given,
because of your constant love and faithfulness.

2 Why should the nations ask us,
  "Where is your God?"
3 Our God is in heaven,
  doing whatever he wishes.
4 Their gods are made of silver and gold,
  formed by human hands.
5 They have mouths, but cannot speak,
  and eyes, but cannot see.
6 They have ears, but cannot hear,
  and noses, but cannot smell.
7 They have hands, but cannot feel,
  and feet, but cannot walk;
  they cannot make a sound.
8 May those who made them and all who
    trust in them,
  become like the idols they have made!

9 Trust in the Lord, people of Israel!
  He helps you and protects you.
10 Trust in the Lord, you priests of God!
  He helps you and protects you.
11 Trust in the Lord, all who fear him!
  He helps you and protects you.

12 The Lord remembers us and will bless us;
  he will bless the people of Israel,
  and all the priests of God.
13 He will bless all who fear him,
  the great and the small alike.

14 May the Lord give you children—
  you and your descendants.
15 May you be blessed by the Lord,
  who made heaven and earth!

16 Heaven belongs to the Lord alone,
  but he gave the earth to men.
17 The Lord is not praised by the dead,
  by any who go down to the land of
    silence.

¹⁸ But we, the living, will give thanks to him,
    now and forever.

Praise the Lord!

A Man Saved from Death Praises God

116 I love the Lord, because he hears
        me;
    he listens to my prayers.
² He listens to me
    every time I call to him.
³ Death drew its ropes tight around me,
    the horrors of the grave closed in on
        me;
    I was filled with fear and anxiety.
⁴ Then I called to the Lord,
    "I beg you, Lord, save me!"

⁵ The Lord is merciful and good;
    our God is compassionate.
⁶ The Lord protects the helpless;
    when I was in danger, he saved me.
⁷ Be confident, my heart,
    because the Lord has been good to me.

⁸ The Lord has saved me from death;
    he stopped my tears
    and kept me from defeat.
⁹ And so I walk in the presence of the Lord
    in the world of the living.
¹⁰ I kept on believing, even when I said,
    "I am completely crushed,"
¹¹ even when I was afraid and said,
    "No one can be trusted."

¹² What can I offer the Lord
    for all his goodness to me?
¹³ I will bring a drink offering to the Lord,
    to thank him for saving me.
¹⁴ In the meeting of all his people,
    I will give him what I have promised.

¹⁵ How painful it is to the Lord,
    when one of his people dies!
¹⁶ I am your servant, Lord;
    I serve you, just as my mother did.
    You have set me free.
¹⁷ I will give you a sacrifice of thanksgiving,
    and offer my prayer to you.
¹⁸⁻¹⁹ In the meeting of all your people,
    in the courts of your temple, in Jeru-
        salem,
    I will give you what I have promised.

Praise the Lord!

In Praise of the Lord

117 Praise the Lord, all nations!
        Praise him, all peoples!
² His constant love for us is strong,
    and his faithfulness is eternal.

Praise the Lord!

A Prayer of Thanks for Victory

118 Give thanks to the Lord, because
        he is good,
    and his love is eternal.
² Let the people of Israel say,
    "His love is eternal."
³ Let the priests of God say,
    "His love is eternal."
⁴ Let all who fear him say,
    "His love is eternal."

⁵ In my distress I called to the Lord;
    he answered me, and set me free.
⁶ The Lord is with me, I will not be afraid;
    what can men do to me?
⁷ It is the Lord who helps me,
    and I will see my enemies defeated.
⁸ It is better to trust in the Lord,

than to depend on men.
9 It is better to trust in the Lord,
than to depend on human leaders.

10 Many enemies were around me;
but I destroyed them by the power of
the Lord!
11 They were around me on every side;
but I destroyed them by the power of
the Lord!
12 They swarmed around me like bees,
but they burned out as quickly as a
brush fire;
by the power of the Lord I destroyed
them!
13 I was fiercely attacked and was being defeated,
but the Lord helped me.
14 The Lord makes me powerful and strong;
he is my Savior!

15 Listen to the glad shouts of victory in the
tents of God's people:
"The Lord's mighty power has done it!
16 His power has brought us victory,
his mighty power in battle!"

17 I will not die, but I will live,
and tell what the Lord has done.
18 He has punished me severely,
but he has not let me die.

19 Open the gates of the temple for me;
I will go in and praise the Lord!

20 This is the gate of the Lord;
only the righteous can come in!

21 I praise you, Lord, because you heard me,
because you have given me victory!

²² The stone which the builders rejected as
worthless,
turned out to be the most important of
all.
²³ This was done by the Lord;
what a wonderful sight it is!
²⁴ What a wonderful day the Lord has given
us;
let us be happy, let us celebrate!
²⁵ Save us, Lord, save us!
Give us success, Lord!

We bless you!

²⁶ God bless him who comes in the name of
the Lord!
From the temple of the Lord we bless
you!
²⁷ The Lord is God; he has been good to us.
With branches in your hands start the
festival
and march around the altar.

²⁸ You are my God, and I give you thanks;
I will proclaim your greatness.

²⁹ Give thanks to the Lord, because he is
   good,
     and his love is eternal.

The Law of the Lord

119 Happy are those whose lives are
          faultless,
     who live according to the law of the
       Lord.
² Happy are those who follow his commands,
     who obey him with all their heart.
³ Surely they do no wrong;
     they walk in the Lord's ways.
⁴ You have given us your laws,
     and told us to obey them faithfully.
⁵ How I hope that I shall be faithful
     in keeping your rules!
⁶ If I pay attention to all your commandments,
     then I will not be disappointed.
⁷ As I learn your righteous rulings,
     I will praise you with a pure heart.
⁸ I will obey your laws;
     don't ever abandon me!

Obedience to the Law of the Lord

⁹ How can a young man keep his life pure?
     By obeying *f* your commands.
¹⁰ With all my heart I try to serve you;
     keep me from disobeying your com-
       mandments!
¹¹ I keep your law in my heart,
     so that I will not sin against you.
¹² I praise you, Lord:
     teach me your rules!
¹³ I will repeat aloud
     all the laws you have given.

f Some ancient translations pure? By obeying; *Hebrew* pure in order
to obey.

¹⁴ I delight in following your commands,
    more than in having great wealth.
¹⁵ I study your instructions;
    I examine your teachings.
¹⁶ I take pleasure in your laws,
    I will not forget your commands.

Happiness in the Law of the Lord

¹⁷ Be good to me, your servant,
    so that I may live and obey your teach-
        ings.
¹⁸ Open my eyes, so that I may see
    the wonderful truths in your law.
¹⁹ I am here on earth for just a little while;
    do not hide your commandments from
        me!
²⁰ My heart aches with longing;
    at all times I want to know your judg-
        ments.
²¹ You reprimand the proud;
    cursed are those who depart from your
        commands.
²² Free me from their insults and scorn,
    because I have kept your laws.
²³ Even though the rulers meet and plot
        against me,
    I, your servant, will study your rules.
²⁴ Your instructions give me pleasure;
    they are my advisers.

Determination to Obey the Law of the Lord

²⁵ I lie defeated in the dust;
    revive me, as you have promised!
²⁶ I confessed all I have done, and you an-
        swered me;
    teach me your rules!
²⁷ Teach me how to obey your laws,
    and I will study your wonderful teach-
        ings.
²⁸ I am overcome by sorrow;
    strengthen me, as you have promised.

²⁹ Keep me from going the wrong way,
    and in your goodness teach me your
    law.
³⁰ I have decided to be obedient;
    I have paid attention to your rules.
³¹ I have followed your instructions, Lord;
    don't let me be disappointed!
³² I will eagerly obey your commands,
    because you will give me more under-
    standing.

A Prayer for Understanding

³³ Teach me, Lord, the meaning of your
    laws,
    and I will obey them at all times.
³⁴ Explain your law to me, and I will obey it;
    I will keep it with all my heart.
³⁵ Lead me in the way of your command-
    ments,
    because in them I find happiness.
³⁶ Make me want to obey your rules,
    rather than to get rich.
³⁷ Keep me from paying attention to what is
    worthless;
    be good to me, as you have promised.
³⁸ Keep your promise to me, your servant,
    which you make to those who fear you.
³⁹ Save me from the insults which I fear;
    how wonderful your rules are!
⁴⁰ I want to obey your commands;
    because you are righteous, be good to
    me!

Trusting the Law of the Lord

⁴¹ Show me how much you love me, Lord,
    and save me according to your promise.
⁴² Then I can answer those who insult me,
    because I trust in your word.
⁴³ Enable me to speak the true message at all
    times,
    because my hope is in your judgments.

44 I will always obey your law,
      forever and ever!
45 I will live in complete freedom,
      because I have tried to obey your rules.
46 I will announce your commands to kings,
      and I will not be ashamed.
47 I find pleasure in obeying your command-
      ments,
      because I love them.
48 I respect and love your commandments;
      I will meditate on your instructions.

Confidence in the Law of the Lord

49 Remember your promise to me, your ser-
      vant;
      it has given me hope.
50 Even in my suffering I was comforted,
      because your promise gave me life.
51 The proud have been scornful of me,
      but I have not departed from your law.
52 I remember the instructions you gave me
      in the past,
      and they bring me comfort, Lord.
53 I am filled with anger,
      when I see the wicked breaking your
      law.
54 Living far from my real home,
      I compose songs about your commands.
55 In the night I think of you, Lord,
      and I obey your law.
56 This is my happiness:
      I obey your commands.

Devotion to the Law of the Lord

57 You are all I want, Lord;
      I promise to obey your laws.
58 I ask you with all my heart:
      have mercy on me, as you have
      promised!
59 I have considered my conduct,
      and promise to follow your rules.

⁶⁰ Without delay, I hurry
     to obey your commandments.
⁶¹ The wicked draw their ropes tight around
     me,
     but I do not forget your law.
⁶² In the middle of the night I wake up
     to praise you for your righteous judg-
     ments.
⁶³ I am a friend of all who serve you,
     of all who obey your laws.
⁶⁴ Lord, the earth is full of your constant
     love;
     teach me your commandments!

The Value of the Law of the Lord

⁶⁵ You have kept your promise, Lord,
     and you are good to me, your servant.
⁶⁶ Give me wisdom and knowledge,
     because I trust in your commands.
⁶⁷ Before you punished me I used to go
     wrong,
     but now I obey your word.
⁶⁸ How good you are, how kind;
     teach me your commands!
⁶⁹ Proud men have told lies about me,
     but with all my heart I obey your rules.
⁷⁰ These men have no understanding,
     but I find pleasure in your law.
⁷¹ My punishment was good for me,
     because it made me learn your com-
     mands.
⁷² The law that you give means more to me
     than all the money in the world.

The Justice of the Law of the Lord

⁷³ You created me, and you keep me safe;
     give me understanding, so that I may
     learn your laws.

74 Those who fear you will be glad when
         they see me,
     because I trust in your promise.
75 I know that your rules are righteous, Lord,
         and that you punished me because you
         are faithful.
76 Let your constant love comfort me,
         as you have promised me, your servant.
77 Have mercy on me, and I will live,
         because I take pleasure in your law.
78 May the proud be ashamed for falsely ac-
         cusing me;
     as for me, I will meditate on your rules.
79 May those who fear you come to me,
         and those who know your commands.
80 May I perfectly obey your command-
         ments,
     and be spared the shame of defeat.

Prayer for Deliverance

81 I am worn out, Lord, waiting for you to
         save me;
     I place my trust in your word.
82 My eyes are tired from watching for what
         you promised,
     while I ask, "When will you help me?"
83 I am as useless as a discarded wineskin;
         yet I have not forgotten your com-
         mands.
84 How much longer do I have to wait?
     When will you punish those who perse-
         cute me?
85 Proud men, who do not obey your law,
         have dug pits to catch me.
86 Your commandments are all trustworthy;
         men persecute me with lies; help me!
87 They have almost succeeded in killing me,
         but I have not neglected your rules.
88 Because of your constant love, be good to
         me,
     so that I may obey your laws.

Faith in the Law of the Lord

⁸⁹ Your word, Lord, will last forever;
   it is firm in heaven.
⁹⁰ Your faithfulness endures through all the
      ages;
   you have set the earth in place and it
      remains.
⁹¹ All things remain to this day because of
      your command,
   because they are all your servants.
⁹² If your law had not been the source of my
      joy,
   I would have died from my punishment.
⁹³ I will never neglect your rules,
   because by them you have kept me
      alive.
⁹⁴ I am yours—save me!
   I have tried to obey your commands.
⁹⁵ Wicked men are waiting to kill me,
   but I will meditate on your laws.
⁹⁶ I have learned that nothing is perfect;
   but your commandment has no limits.

Love for the Law of the Lord

⁹⁷ How I love your law!
   I think about it all day long.
⁹⁸ Your commandment is with me all the
      time,
   and makes me wiser than all my ene-
      mies.
⁹⁹ I understand more than all my teachers,
   because I think on your instructions.
¹⁰⁰ I have greater wisdom than old men,
   because I obey your commands.
¹⁰¹ I have avoided all evil conduct,
   because I want to obey your word.
¹⁰² I have not neglected your instructions,
   because it was you who taught me.
¹⁰³ How sweet is the taste of your rules;
   they are sweeter than honey!
¹⁰⁴ I gain wisdom from your laws,
   and so I hate all bad conduct.

A light for my path

Light from the Law of the Lord

¹⁰⁵ Your word is a lamp to guide me,
   and a light for my path.
¹⁰⁶ I will keep my solemn promise
   to obey your righteous instructions.
¹⁰⁷ My sufferings, Lord, are terrible indeed;
   keep me alive, as you have promised!
¹⁰⁸ Accept my prayer of thanks, Lord,
   and teach me your commands.
¹⁰⁹ I am always ready to risk my life;
   I have not forgotten your law.
¹¹⁰ Wicked men lay a trap for me,
   but I have not disobeyed your commands.
¹¹¹ Your commandments are my eternal possession;
   they are the joy of my heart.
¹¹² I have decided to obey your rules,
   until the day I die.

Safety in the Law of the Lord

¹¹³ I hate those who are not loyal to you,
   but I love your law.
¹¹⁴ You are my defender and protector;
   I hope in your promise.
¹¹⁵ Go away from me, you sinful people!
   I will obey the commandments of my
      God.
¹¹⁶ Give me strength, as you promised, and I
      shall live;
   don't let me be disappointed in my
      hope!
¹¹⁷ Hold me, and I will be safe,
   and I will always pay attention to your
      commands.
¹¹⁸ You reject all who disobey your laws;
   their deceitful schemes are useless.
¹¹⁹ You treat all the wicked like rubbish,
   and so I love your instructions.
¹²⁰ Because of you, I am afraid;
   I am filled with fear because of your
      judgments.

Obedience to the Law of the Lord

¹²¹ I have done what is right and good;
   don't abandon me to my enemies!
¹²² Promise that you will help your servant;
   don't let proud men trouble me!
¹²³ My eyes are tired from watching for your
      salvation,
   for the deliverance you promised.
¹²⁴ Treat me according to your constant love,
   and teach me your commands.
¹²⁵ I am your servant, so give me understand-
      ing
   that I may know your teachings.
¹²⁶ Lord, it is time for you to act,
   because people are disobeying your
      law!
¹²⁷ I love your commands more than gold,
   more than the finest gold.

128 And so I follow^g all your instructions;
 I hate all wrong ways.

Desire to Obey the Law of the Lord

129 Your teachings are wonderful;
 I obey them with all my heart.
130 The explanation of your teachings gives
  light,
 and brings wisdom to the inexperi-
  enced.
131 With open mouth I pant,
 in my desire for your commands.
132 Turn to me and have mercy on me
 as you do on those who love you.
133 Keep me from falling, as you have promised;
 don't let me be overcome by evil.
134 Save me from those who oppress me,
 so that I may obey your commands.
135 Bless me with your presence,
 and teach me your laws.
136 My tears pour down like a river,
 because people do not obey your law.

The Justice of the Law of the Lord

137 You are righteous, Lord,
 and your laws are right.
138 The rules that you have given
 are completely fair and right.
139 My anger burns in me like a fire,
 because my enemies disregard your
  commands.
140 How certain your promise is!
 How much your servant loves it!
141 I am unimportant and despised,
 but I do not neglect your rules.
142 Your righteousness will last forever,
 and your law is always true.
143 I am filled with trouble and distress,

gSome ancient translations I follow; Hebrew uncertain.

but your commandments bring me joy.
¹⁴⁴ Your instructions are righteous forever;
give me understanding, and I shall live.

Prayer for Deliverance

¹⁴⁵ With all my heart I call to you;
answer me, Lord, and I will obey your
commands!
¹⁴⁶ I call to you;
save me, and I will follow your rules!
¹⁴⁷ Before sunrise I call to you for help;
I place my hope in your promise.
¹⁴⁸ All night long I lie awake,
to meditate on your instructions.
¹⁴⁹ Hear me, Lord, according to your con-
stant love;
preserve my life, according to your
goodness!
¹⁵⁰ My cruel persecutors are coming closer,
people who never keep your law.
¹⁵¹ But you are near to me, Lord,
and all your promises are true.
¹⁵² Long ago I learned about your instruc-
tions;
you made them to last forever.

Plea for Salvation

¹⁵³ Look at my suffering, and save me,
because I have not neglected your law.
¹⁵⁴ Defend my cause, and set me free;
save me, as you have promised!
¹⁵⁵ The wicked will not be saved,
because they do not obey your laws;
¹⁵⁶ but your compassion, Lord, is great,
so save me, according to your decision.
¹⁵⁷ I have many enemies and oppressors,
but I do not fail to obey your laws.
¹⁵⁸ When I look at those traitors, I am filled
with disgust,
because they do not obey your command.

¹⁵⁹ See how I love your instructions, Lord!
Save me, according to your constant
love.
¹⁶⁰ The heart of your law is truth,
and all your righteous rules are eternal.

Dedication to the Law of the Lord

¹⁶¹ Powerful men attack me unjustly,
but it is your law that I respect.
¹⁶² How happy I am because of your prom-
ises,
as happy as someone who finds rich
treasure.
¹⁶³ I hate and detest all lies,
but I love your law.
¹⁶⁴ Seven times each day I thank you
for your righteous judgments.
¹⁶⁵ Those who love your law have complete
security,
and there is nothing that can make
them fall.
¹⁶⁶ I wait for you to save me, Lord,
and I do what you command.
¹⁶⁷ I obey your rules;
I love them with all my heart.
¹⁶⁸ I obey your commands and your instruc-
tions;
you see everything I do.

A Prayer for Help

¹⁶⁹ Let my cry for help reach you, Lord!
Give me understanding, as you have
promised.
¹⁷⁰ Let my prayer come before you,
and save me, according to your promise!
¹⁷¹ I will always praise you,
because you teach me your rules.
¹⁷² I will sing about your law,
because your commands are just.
¹⁷³ Be always ready to help me,

because I follow your commands.
¹⁷⁴ How I long for your salvation, Lord!
    I find happiness in your law.
¹⁷⁵ Give me life, so that I may praise you;
    may your instructions help me!
¹⁷⁶ I wander about like a lost sheep;
    so come and look for me, your servant,
    because I have not neglected your laws.

A Prayer for Help

120 When I was in trouble I called to
        the Lord,
    and he answered me.
² Save me, Lord,
    from liars and deceivers!

³ You liars, what will God do to you?
    How will he punish you?
⁴ With a soldier's sharp arrows,
    with red-hot charcoals!

⁵ Living among you is as bad as living in
      Meshech,
    or among the people of Kedar!
⁶ I have lived too long
    with people who hate peace!
⁷ When I speak of peace,
    they are for war.

The Lord Our Protector

121 I look to the mountains;
      where will my help come from?
² My help comes from the Lord,
    who made heaven and earth.

³ May he not let me fall;
    may my protector keep awake!

⁴ The protector of Israel
    does not doze or sleep!
⁵ The Lord will guard you;
    he is by your side to protect you.
⁶ The sun will not hurt you during the day,
    nor the moon during the night.

⁷ The Lord will protect you from all danger;
    he will keep you safe.
⁸ He will protect you as you come and go,
    from now on and forever.

In Praise of Jerusalem

122 I was glad when they said to me,
        "Let us go to the Lord's house!"
² And now we are here,
    standing inside the gates of Jerusalem!

³ Jerusalem is a city restored
    in beautiful order and harmony!
⁴ This is where the tribes come,
    the tribes of Israel,
  to give thanks to the Lord,
    as he commanded them.
⁵ This is where the law courts are,
    where the king judges his people.

⁶ Pray for the peace of Jerusalem!
    "May those who love you prosper!
⁷   May there be peace inside your walls,
    and safety in your palaces."
⁸ For the sake of my friends and compan-
    ions,
      I say to Jerusalem, "Peace be with
      you!"
⁹ For the sake of the house of the Lord, our
    God,
      I pray for your prosperity.

A Prayer for Mercy

123 Lord, I look up to you,
    up to heaven, where you rule.
2 As the servant depends on his master,
    and the maid depends on her mistress,
so we keep looking to you, Lord our God,
    until you have mercy on us.

3 Be merciful to us, Lord, be merciful;
    we have been treated with so much con-
        tempt!
4 We have been mocked too long by the
    rich,
        and scorned by proud oppressors!

God the Savior of His People

124 What if the Lord had not been on
    our side?
    Answer, Israel!
2 "If the Lord had not been on our side,
    when our enemies attacked us,
3 then they would have swallowed us alive,
    in their furious anger against us;
4 then the flood would have carried us
    away,
        the water would have drowned us,
5   the raging torrent would have drowned
    us."

6 Let us thank the Lord,
    who has not let our enemies destroy us.
7 We have escaped like a bird from the hun-
    ter's trap;
        the trap has been broken, and we are
        free!
8 Our help comes from the Lord,
    who made heaven and earth.

The Security of God's People

125 Those who trust in the Lord are
like Mount Zion,
which can never be shaken, never be
moved.
2 As the mountains surround Jerusalem,
so the Lord surrounds his people,
from now on and forever.

3 The wicked will not always rule over the
land of God's people;
if they did, God's people themselves
might do evil.
4 Lord, do good to those who are good,
to those who obey your commands!
5 But punish those who follow their own
wicked ways,
when you punish the evildoers!

Peace be with Israel!

A Prayer for Deliverance

126 When the Lord brought us back
to Zion,
it was like a dream!
2 How we laughed, how we sang for joy!
Then the other nations said about us,
"The Lord did great things for them!"
3 Indeed he did great things for us;
how happy we were!

4 Lord, take us back to our land,
just as your rain brings water back to
dry riverbeds.
5 Let those who cried while they planted,
gather the harvest with joy!

6 Those who cried as they went out carrying
the seed
will come back singing for joy,
bringing in the harvest!

Gather the harvest with joy!

In Praise of God's Goodness

127 If the Lord does not build the
house,
the work of the builders is useless;
if the Lord does not protect the city,
it does no good for the sentries to stand
guard.
² It is useless to work so hard for a living,
getting up early and going to bed late,
because the Lord gives rest to those he
loves.

³ Children are a gift from the Lord;
they are a real blessing.
⁴ The sons a man has when he is young
are like arrows in a soldier's hand.
⁵ Happy is the man who has many such
arrows!
He will never be defeated.

when he meets his enemies in the place
of judgment.

The Reward of Obedience to the Lord

128 Happy are those who fear the
Lord,
who live by his commands!
2 You will earn enough to provide for your
needs;
you will be happy and prosperous.
3 Your wife will be like a fruitful vine in
your home,
and your sons will be like young olive
trees around your table.
4 A man who obeys the Lord
will surely be blessed like this.

5 May the Lord bless you from Zion!
May you see Jerusalem prosper
all the days of your life!
6 May you live to see your grandchildren!

Peace be with Israel!

Prayer against Israel's Enemies

129 Israel, tell how cruelly your enemies have persecuted you
ever since you were young!
2 "Ever since I was young,
my enemies have persecuted me cruelly,
but they have not overcome me.
3 They cut deep wounds in my back,
and made it like a plowed field.
4 But the Lord, the righteous one,
has freed me from slavery."

5 May all who hate Zion
be defeated and driven back!
6 May they be like grass growing on the
housetops,

that dries up before it can be cut.
7 No one gathers it up,
or carries it away in bundles.
8 No one who passes by will say,
"May the Lord bless you!
We bless you in the name of the Lord!"

A Prayer for Help

130 In my despair I call to you, Lord.
2 Hear my cry, Lord,
listen to my call for help!
3 If you kept a record of our sins,
who could escape being condemned?
4 But you forgive us,
so that we should fear you.

5 I wait eagerly for the Lord's help,
and in his word I trust.
6 I wait for the Lord,
more eagerly than watchmen wait for
the dawn,
· than watchmen wait for the dawn.

7 Israel, trust in the Lord,
because his love is constant,
and he is always willing to save.
8 He will save his people Israel
from all their sins.

A Prayer of Humble Trust

131 Lord, I have given up my pride,
and turned from my arrogance.
I am not concerned with great matters,
or with subjects too difficult for me.
2 But I am content and at peace.
As a child lies quietly in its mother's arms,
so my heart is quiet within me.
3 Israel, trust in the Lord,
from now on and forever!

132 Lord, do not forget David
and all the work he did.

2 Remember, Lord, what he promised,
the vow he made to you, the Mighty
God of Israel:

3 "I will not go home or go to bed;

4 I will not rest or sleep,

5 until I provide a place for the Lord,
a home for the Mighty God of Israel."

6 We heard about the covenant box in Beth-
lehem,
and found it in the fields of Jaar.

7 We said, "Let us go to the Lord's house;
let us worship before his throne!"

8 Come to your resting place, Lord, with
the covenant box,
the symbol of your power.

9 May the priests proclaim that you save
your people;
may all your people shout for joy!

10 You made a promise to your servant David;
do not reject your chosen king, Lord!

11 You made a solemn promise to David,
and you will not take it back:
"I will make one of your sons king,
and he will rule after you.

12 If your sons are true to my covenant,
and to the commands I give them,
their sons, also, will follow you as kings
for all time."

13 The Lord has chosen Zion;
he wants to make his home there:

14 "This is where I will live forever;
this is where I want to rule.

15 I will richly provide Zion with all she
needs;

I will satisfy her poor with food.
¹⁶ I will have her priests proclaim that I save,
   and her people will sing and shout for
      joy.
¹⁷ Here I will make one of David's descend-
      ants a great king;
   here I will preserve the rule of my
      chosen king.
¹⁸ I will cover his enemies with shame,
   but his kingdom will prosper and flour-
      ish."

In Praise of Brotherly Love

133 How wonderful it is, how pleasant,
         for God's people to live together
            like brothers!
² It is like the precious olive oil
   running down from Aaron's head and
      beard,
   down to the collar of his robes.
³ It is like the dew on Mount Hermon,
   falling on the hills of Zion.
That is where the Lord has promised his
      blessing,
   life that never ends.

A Call to Praise God

134 Come, praise the Lord,
         all his servants,
      all who serve in his temple at night.
² Raise your hands in prayer in the temple,
   and praise the Lord!

³ May the Lord, who made heaven and
      earth,
   bless you from Zion.

A Hymn of Praise

135 Praise the Lord!

Praise his name, you servants of the Lord,
2 who stand in the Lord's house,
   in the sanctuary of our God.
3 Praise the Lord, because he is good;
   sing praises to his name, because he is
      kind.
4 He chose Jacob for himself,
   the people of Israel for his own.

5 I know that our Lord is great;
   he is greater than all the gods.
6 He does whatever he wishes
   in heaven and on earth,
   in the seas and in the depths below.
7 He brings storm clouds from the ends of
      the earth;
   he makes lightning for the storms,
   and brings out the wind from his store-
      room.

8 In Egypt he killed all the firstborn
   of both men and animals.
9 There he performed miracles and wonders
   to punish Pharaoh and all his officials.
10 He destroyed many nations,
   and killed powerful kings:
11 Sihon, king of the Amorites,
   Og, king of Bashan,
   and all the kings in Canaan.
12 He gave their land to his people;
   he gave it to Israel.

13 Lord, men will always know that you are
      God;
   all generations will remember you.
14 The Lord will take pity on his people;
   he will set his servants free.

¹⁵ The idols of the nations are made of silver
      and gold;
      they are formed by human hands.
¹⁶ They have mouths, but cannot speak,
      and eyes, but cannot see.
¹⁷ They have ears, but cannot hear;
      there is no breath in their mouths.
¹⁸ May those who made them and all who
      trust in them
      become like the idols they have made!

¹⁹ Praise the Lord, people of Israel;
      praise him, you priests of God!
²⁰ Praise the Lord, you Levites;
      praise him, all you that fear him!
²¹ Praise the Lord in Zion,
      in Jerusalem, his home.

Praise the Lord!

A Hymn of Thanksgiving

136   Give thanks to the Lord, because
        he is good,
      and his love is eternal.
² Give thanks to the greatest of all gods;
      his love is eternal.
³ Give thanks to the mightiest of all lords;
      his love is eternal.

⁴ He alone does great miracles;
      his love is eternal.
⁵ By his wisdom he made the heavens;
      his love is eternal;
⁶ he built the earth on the deep waters;
      his love is eternal.
⁷ He made the sun and the moon;
      his love is eternal;
⁸ the sun to rule over the day;
      his love is eternal;

⁹ the moon and the stars to rule over the
   night;
   his love is eternal.

¹⁰ He killed the firstborn sons of the
   Egyptians;
   his love is eternal.
¹¹ He led the people of Israel out of Egypt;
   his love is eternal;
¹² with his strong hand, his powerful arm;
   his love is eternal.
¹³ He divided the Sea of Reeds;
   his love is eternal;
¹⁴ he led his people through it;
   his love is eternal;
¹⁵ he drowned Pharaoh and his army;
   his love is eternal.

¹⁶ He led his people in the desert;
   his love is eternal.
¹⁷ He killed powerful kings;
   his love is eternal;
¹⁸ he killed famous kings;
   his love is eternal;
¹⁹ Sihon, king of the Amorites;
   his love is eternal;
²⁰ and Og, king of Bashan;
   his love is eternal.
²¹ He gave their land to his people;
   his love is eternal;
²² he gave it to Israel, his servant;
   his love is eternal.

²³ He did not forget us when we were defeated;
   his love is eternal;
²⁴ he freed us from our enemies;
   his love is eternal.
²⁵ He gives food to all men and animals;
   his love is eternal.

²⁶ Give thanks to the God of heaven;
   his love is eternal.

The Lament of Israelites in Exile

137 By the rivers of Babylon
we sat and cried when we
remembered Zion.
2 On the willows nearby
we hung our harps.
3 Those who captured us told us to sing;
they told us to entertain them:
"Sing us a song about Zion!"

4 How can we sing the Lord's song
in a foreign land?
5 May I never be able to play the harp again,
if I forget you, Jerusalem!
6 May I never be able to sing again,
if I do not remember you,
if I do not think of you as my greatest
joy!

7 Remember, Lord, what the Edomites did,
the day Jerusalem was captured.
Remember how they kept saying,
"Tear it down to the ground!"
8 Babylon, you will be destroyed!
Happy is the man who pays you back
for what you have done to us—
9 who takes your babies,
and smashes them on a rock!

A Prayer of Thanksgiving

138 I thank you, Lord, with all my
heart;
I sing praise to you before the gods.
2 I bow down in front of your holy temple
and praise your name,
because of your constant love and faithfulness,
because you have shown that you and
your commands are supreme.*h*

*h*shown that you and your commands are supreme; *Hebrew* shown that
your command is greater than all your name.

3 You answered me when I called to you;
    with your strength you strengthened
      me.

4 All the kings of the earth will praise you,
      Lord,
    because they have heard your promises.
5 They will sing about what the Lord has
      done,
    and about his great glory.
6 Even though the Lord is so high above,
    he cares for the lowly,
    and the proud cannot hide from him.

7 Even when I am surrounded by troubles,
    you keep me safe;
  you oppose my angry enemies,
    and save me by your power.
8 You will do everything you have prom-
      ised me;
    Lord, your love is constant forever.
    Complete the work that you have
    begun.

God's Complete Knowledge and Care

139 Lord, you have examined me, and
        you know me.
2 You know everything I do;
    from far away you understand all my
      thoughts.
3 You see me, whether I am working or
      resting;
    you know all my actions.
4 Even before I speak
    you already know what I will say.
5 You are all around me, on every side;
    you protect me with your power.
6 Your knowledge of me is overwhelming;
    it is too deep for me to understand.

7 Where could I go to escape from your
        spirit?
    Where could I get away from your pres-
        ence?
8 If I went up to heaven, you would be
        there;
    if I lay down in the world of the dead,
        you would be there.
9 If I flew away beyond the east,
    or lived in the farthest place in the west,
10 you would be there to lead me,
    you would be there to help me.
11 I could ask the darkness to hide me,
    or the light around me to turn into
        night,
12 but even the darkness is not dark for you,
    and the night is as bright as the day.
    Darkness and light are the same to you.

13 You created every part of me;
    you put me together in my mother's
        womb.
14 I praise you because you are to be feared;
    all you do is strange and wonderful.
    I know it with all my heart.
15 You saw my bones being formed,
    carefully put together in my mother's
        womb,
    when I was growing there in secret.
16 You saw me before I was born.
    The days that had been created for me
        had all been recorded in your book,
    before any of them had ever begun.
17 God, how difficult your thoughts are for
        me;
    how many of them there are!
18 If I counted them, they would be more
        than the grains of sand.
    When I awake, I am still with you.

19 God, how I wish you would kill the
        wicked!

How I wish violent men would leave me
   alone!
20 They say wicked things about you;
   they speak evil things against your
      name.[i]
21 Lord, how I hate those who hate you!
   How I despise those who rebel against
      you!
22 My hatred for them is complete;
   I regard them as my enemies.

23 Examine me, God, and know my mind;
   test me, and discover my thoughts.
24 Find out if there is any deceit in me,
   and guide me in the eternal way.

A Prayer for Protection

140 Save me, Lord, from evil men;
   keep me safe from violent men.
2 They are always plotting evil,
   always stirring up quarrels.
3 Their tongues are like deadly snakes,
   their words are like a cobra's poison.

4 Protect me, Lord, from the power of the
      wicked;
   keep me safe from violent men,
   who plot my downfall.
5 Proud men have laid a trap for me;
   they have spread a net of ropes,
   and along the path they have set traps
      to catch me.

6 I say to the Lord, "You are my God."
   Hear my cry for help, Lord!
7 Lord, my God, my strong Savior,
   you have protected me in battle.
8 Lord, don't give the wicked what they
      want;
   don't let their evil plots succeed!

[i]*Hebrew unclear.*

⁹ Don't let my enemies be victorious;*J*
    make their threats against me fall back
      on them.
¹⁰ May red-hot coals fall on them;
    may they be thrown into a pit and never
      get out.
¹¹ May those who accuse others falsely not
      succeed;
    may evil overtake the violent man and
      destroy him.

¹² I know that you, Lord, defend the cause of
      the poor,
    and the rights of the needy.
¹³ The righteous will praise you indeed;
    they will live in your presence.

An Evening Prayer

141 I call to you, Lord; help me now!
    Listen to me when I call to you.
² Receive my prayer as incense,
    my uplifted hands as an evening sac-
      rifice.

³ Lord, place a guard at my mouth,
    a sentry at the door of my lips.
⁴ Keep me from wanting to do wrong,
    or to join evil men in their wickedness.
May I never take part in their feasts!

⁵ A good man may punish me and repri-
      mand me in kindness,
    but I will not let an evil man anoint my
      head,
    because I am always praying against his
      evil deeds.
⁶ When their rulers are thrown down on
    rocky cliffs,

*J*Don't let my enemies be victorious; *Hebrew unclear.*

the people will admit that my words
    were true.
⁷ Like wood that is split and chopped into
    bits,
    so their bones are scattered at the edge
    of the grave.ᵏ

⁸ But I, Lord God, keep trusting in you;
    I seek your protection;
    don't let me die!
⁹ Protect me from the traps they have set
    for me,
    from the snares of those evildoers.
¹⁰ May the wicked fall into their own traps,
    while I go by unharmed.

A Prayer for Helpˡ

142   I call to the Lord for help;
         I plead with him.
² I bring him all my complaints;
    I tell him all my troubles.
³ When I am ready to give up,
    he knows what I should do.
In the path where I walk
    my enemies have hidden a trap for me.
⁴ I look beside me and I see
    that there is no one to help me;
there is no one to protect me;
    no one cares for me.

⁵ Lord, I cry to you for help;
    you, Lord, are my protector;
    you are all I want in this life.
⁶ Listen to my cry for help,
    because I am sunk in despair.
Save me from my enemies,
    who are much stronger than I am.
⁷ Rescue me from my trouble;

ᵏ *Verses 5–7 in Hebrew are unclear.*   ˡ*Hebrew title:* A prayer of David
when he was in the cave.

then in the meeting of your people I will
   praise you,
because you have been good to me.

A Prayer for Help

143 Lord, hear my prayer,
            listen to my plea!
You are righteous and faithful,
      so answer me!
2 Don't put me, your servant, on trial;
      no one is innocent in your sight.

3 My enemy has persecuted me,
      and completely defeated me.
He has put me in a dark prison,
      and I am like those who died long ago.
4 So I am ready to give up;
      I am in deep despair.

5 I remember the days gone by;
      I think about all that you have done,
      I bring to mind all your deeds.
6 I lift up my hands to you in prayer;
      like dry ground my soul thirsts for you.

7 Answer me now, Lord!
      I have lost all hope!
Don't hide yourself from me,
      or I will be among those who go down
         to the land of the dead.
8 I trust in you;
      in the morning remind me of your con-
         stant love.
My prayers go up to you;
      show me the way I should go.

9 I go to you for protection, Lord;
      rescue me from my enemies.
10 You are my God;
      teach me to do your will.
May your spirit be good to me
      and guide me on a safe path.

¹¹ Save me, Lord, as you have promised;
in your goodness, rescue me from my
troubles!
¹² In your love for me, kill my enemies,
and destroy all my oppressors,
because I am your servant.

A King Thanks God for Victory

144 Praise the Lord, my protector;
he trains me for battle,
and prepares me for war.
² He is my protector*m* and defender,
my shelter and Savior,
in whom I trust for safety.
He subdues the nations under me.

³ Lord, what is man, that you notice him;
mere man, that you pay attention to
him?
⁴ He is like a puff of wind;
his days are like a passing shadow.

⁵ Lord, pull back the sky, and come down;
touch the mountains, and they will pour
out smoke.
⁶ Send flashes of lightning, and scatter your
enemies;
shoot your arrows, and send them running!
⁷ Reach down from above,
pull me out of the deep water, and save
me;
save me from the power of foreigners,
⁸ who never tell the truth,
and lie even under oath.

⁹ I will sing you a new song, God;
I will play the harp and sing to you.
¹⁰ You give victory to kings,

*m*protector *(as in Ps. 18.2 and 2 Sam. 22.2); Hebrew* love.

and rescue your servant David.
11 Save me from my cruel enemies,
rescue me from the power of foreigners,
who never tell the truth,
and lie even under oath.

12 May our sons in their youth
be like plants that grow up strong.
May our daughters be like statues,
which adorn the corners of a palace.
13 May our barns be filled
with crops of every kind.
May the sheep in our fields
bear young by the tens of thousands.
14 May our cattle reproduce plentifully,
without miscarriage or loss.
May there be no cries of distress in our
streets!

15 Happy is the nation of whom this is true;
happy are the people whose God is the
Lord!

A Hymn of Praise

145 I will proclaim your greatness, my
God and king;
I will thank you forever and ever.
2 Every day I will thank you;
I will praise you forever and ever.
3 The Lord is great, and must be highly
praised;
his greatness is beyond understanding.

4 What you have done will be praised from
one generation to the next;
they will proclaim your mighty acts.
5 Men will speak of your glory and majesty,
and I will meditate on your wonderful
deeds.

⁶ Men will speak of your mighty acts,
     and I will proclaim your greatness.
⁷ They will tell about all your goodness,
     and sing about your kindness.

⁸ The Lord is loving and merciful,
     slow to become angry and full of con-
        stant love.
⁹ He is good to everyone
     and has compassion on all he made.

¹⁰ All your creatures, Lord, will praise you,
     and your people will give you thanks!
¹¹ They will speak of the glory of your king-
        dom,
     and tell of your might,
¹² so that all men will know your mighty
        acts,
     and the glorious majesty of your king-
        dom.
¹³ Your kingdom is eternal,
     and you are king forever.

The Lord is faithful to his promises,
     and good in all he does.
¹⁴ He helps all who are in trouble;
     he raises all who are humbled.
¹⁵ All living things look hopefully to him,
     and he gives them food when they need
        it.
¹⁶ He gives them enough
     and satisfies the needs of all.
¹⁷ The Lord is righteous in all he does,
     merciful in all his acts.
¹⁸ He is near to all who call to him,
     who call to him with sincerity.
¹⁹ He supplies the needs of all who fear him;
     he hears their cry and saves them.
²⁰ He protects all who love him,
     but he will destroy all the wicked.

²¹ I will always praise the Lord;
    let all creatures praise his holy name
      forever!

In Praise of God the Savior

146 Praise the Lord!
    Praise the Lord, my soul!
² I will praise him as long as I live;
    I will sing to my God all my life.

³ Don't put your trust in human leaders,
    or anyone else who cannot save you.
⁴ When they die they return to the soil;
    on that day all their plans come to an
      end.

⁵ Happy is the man who has the God of
      Jacob to help him,
    and depends on the Lord his God,
⁶ who created heaven, earth, and sea,
    and all that is in them.
He always keeps his promises;
  ⁷ he judges in favor of the oppressed
    and gives food to the hungry.

The Lord sets prisoners free
  ⁸ and gives sight to the blind.
He raises all who are humbled;
    he loves his righteous people.
⁹ He protects the foreigners who live in the
      land;
    he helps widows and orphans,
    but ruins the plans of the wicked.

¹⁰ The Lord will be king forever!
    Your God, Zion, will reign for all time!

Praise the Lord!

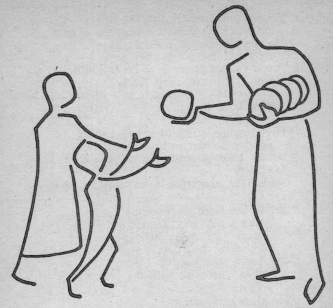

And gives food to the hungry

In Praise of God the Almighty

147 Praise the Lord!

It is good to sing praise to our God;
    it is pleasant and right to praise him.
2 The Lord is restoring Jerusalem;
    he is bringing back the exiles.
3 He heals the brokenhearted,
    and bandages their wounds.

4 He has determined the number of the
    stars
    and calls each one by name.
5 Great and almighty is our Lord;
    his knowledge cannot be measured.
6 He raises the humble,
    but crushes the wicked to the ground.

7 Sing hymns of praise to the Lord;
    play music to our God on the harp.
8 He spreads clouds over the sky;
    he provides rain for the earth,
    and makes grass grow on the hills.
9 He gives animals their food,
    and feeds the young ravens when they
        call.

10 His pleasure is not in strong horses,
    nor his delight in brave soldiers;
11 but he takes pleasure in those who fear
        him,
    in those who trust in his constant love.

12 Praise the Lord, Jerusalem!
    Praise your God, Zion!
13 He keeps your gates strong;
    he blesses your people.
14 He keeps your borders safe
    and satisfies you with the best wheat.

15 He gives an order,
    and it comes quickly to the earth.
16 He sends snow as thick as wool,
    and scatters frost like dust.
17 He sends hail like gravel;
    no one can endure the cold he sends!
18 Then he gives a command, and melts the
        ice,
    he sends the wind, and the water flows.

19 He gives his message to Jacob,
    his instructions and laws to Israel.
20 He has not done this for other nations;
    they do not know his laws.

    Praise the Lord!

A Call for the Universe to Praise God

148 Praise the Lord!

Praise the Lord from heaven,
  you that live in the heights above!
2 Praise him, all his angels,
  all his heavenly armies!

3 Praise him, sun and moon;
  praise him, shining stars!
4 Praise him, highest heavens,
  and the waters above the sky!

5 Let them all praise the name of the Lord!
He commanded, and they were created;
6   by his command they were fixed in their
      places forever,
  and they cannot disobey.

7 Praise the Lord from the earth,
  sea monsters and all ocean depths;
8 lightning and hail, snow and clouds,
  strong winds that obey his command!

9 Praise him, hills and mountains,
  fruit trees and forests;
10 all animals, tame and wild,
  reptiles and birds!

11 Praise him, kings and all peoples,
  princes and all other rulers;
12 young men and girls,
  old people and children also!

13 Let them all praise the name of the Lord.
His name is greater than all others;
  his glory is above earth and heaven!
14 He made his nation strong,

so that all his people praise him,
the people of Israel, so dear to him!

Praise the Lord!

A Hymn of Praise

149   Praise the Lord!

Sing a new song to the Lord;
    praise him in the meeting of his faithful
    people!
2 Be glad, Israel, because of your creator;
    rejoice, people of Zion, because of your
    king!
3 Praise his name with dancing;
    play drums and harps in praise of him.

4 The Lord takes pleasure in his people;
    he honors the humble with victory.
5 Let God's people rejoice in their triumph,
    and sing joyfully at their feasts.
6 Let them shout aloud as they praise God,
    with their sharp swords in their hands,
7 to defeat the nations,
    and to punish the peoples;
8 to tie up their kings in chains,
    their leaders in chains of iron;
9 to punish the nations as God has com-
    manded.
    This is the victory of God's people!

Praise the Lord!

Praise the Lord!

150   Praise the Lord!

Praise God in his temple!
    Praise his strength in heaven!

² Praise him for the mighty things he has
        done!
    Praise his supreme greatness!

³ Praise him with trumpets!
    Praise him with harps and lyres!
⁴ Praise him with drums and dancing!
    Praise him with harps and flutes!
⁵ Praise him with cymbals!
    Praise him with loud cymbals!
⁶ Praise the Lord, all living creatures!

    Praise the Lord!

Praise the Lord!

MAPS

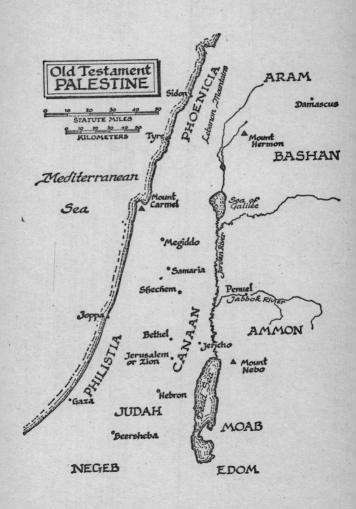

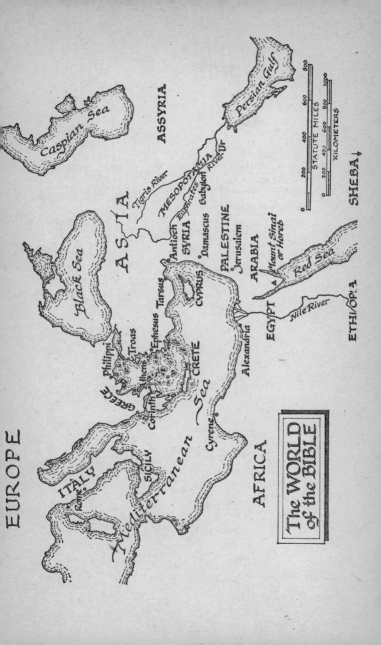

NOTES